OData
And
Visual Studio LightSwitch
Using ASP.NET / Windows Phone /
jQuery / datajs / Knockout

Copyright

Table of Contents

Dedication

As always, for Valerie and Zachary

Preface

Requirements

You must have Visual Studio LightSwitch in Visual Studio Professional 2012 (or higher) to create the applications described in this book. Visual Studio LightSwitch 2011 is the previous version of LightSwitch, and will not meet this requirement.

Intended Audience

You are familiar with, and you are creating applications using Visual Studio LightSwitch (http://www.microsoft.com/visualstudio/en-us/lightswitch).

If you are new to using LightSwitch, it is suggested that you start with this tutorial:

http://lightswitchhelpwebsite.com/Blog/tabid/61/EntryId/12/Online-Ordering-System-An-End-To-End-LightSwitch-Example.aspx

You do not need to have prior experience or knowledge of OData, jQuery, Windows Phone, datajs, or Knockout.

Thank You

Microsoft:

Beth Massi
Eric Erhardt
Matt Sampson
Matt Thalman
Dan Leeaphon
Andrew Lader
Karol Zadora-Przylecki
Steve Hoag
Sheel Shah
Joe Binder
Michael Eng
Robert Green
John Rivard
Steve Anonsen
John Stallo
Jay Schmelzer

LightSwitch Superstars:

Richard Waddell
Delordson Kallon
Jan Van der Haegen
Alessandro Del Sole
Rich Dudley
Dan Beall
Paul Patterson
Kostas Christodoulou
Andrew Brust
Stephen J Naughton
Garth Henderson
Jewel Lambert
Robert MacLean
Bill Quinn

Chapter 1: What Is This Book About?

This book is about Microsoft Visual Studio LightSwitch and OData. The purpose of this book is to demonstrate its use, and explain its importance.

What Is Visual Studio LightSwitch?

Visual Studio LightSwitch is a development tool that provides the easiest and fastest way to create 'forms over data, line of business applications'. It allows you to build applications for the desktop and the cloud. It does this by allowing you to quickly and easily define and connect to your data, program your security and business rules, and expose this via OData to practically any 'client' such as mobile devices and web pages.

What Is OData?

OData is a protocol used to expose and consume data over the web. It uses a common REST-like (representational state transfer) interface to communicate, rather than the usual pre-defined application specific interfaces used by traditional web services. OData is a project created by Microsoft. The home page for the project is at: http://www.odata.org.

As described in the article: **LightSwitch Architecture: OData (John Rivard)** (http://blogs.msdn.com/b/lightswitch/archive/2012/03/22/lightswitch-architecture-odata.aspx), OData allows CRUD (**C**reate, **R**ead, **U**pdate, **D**elete) operations using the following HTTP (**H**ypertext **T**ransfer **P**rotocol) verbs:

- Create: **POST**
- Read: **GET**
- Update: **PUT**
- Delete: **DELETE**

This allows you to have full data interaction when you use OData. In addition, OData provides a mechanism to query the data. For example, in subsequent chapters we will demonstrate how a mobile application is able to query for orders for a specific customer. This is done without the need to define a "get customer orders" web service. We simply use the standard OData protocol.

OData is Communication with Clients and Servers Outside of Your LightSwitch Application

Communication between your LightSwitch application, and clients that need to communicate with it, is very important. For example, allowing a user to place orders in your LightSwitch application using a mobile phone or a tablet is an important component to creating productive applications for your end users.

OData Allows You to Centralize Your Business Rules and Security

Secrurity is an important aspect of your application. Using LightSwitch, you are able to easily configure security.

The following code restricts a non-administrator from accessing any order that is not their own:

```
partial void FlowerShopOrders_Filter(ref Expression<Func<FlowerShopOrder, bool>> filter)
{
    if(!this.Application.User.HasPermission(Permissions.SecurityAdministration))
    {
        filter = e => e.FlowerShopCustomer.Username == this.Application.User.Name;
    }
}
```

This code needs to be implemented only once to protect the data and to enforce the business rule, no matter what client is being used.

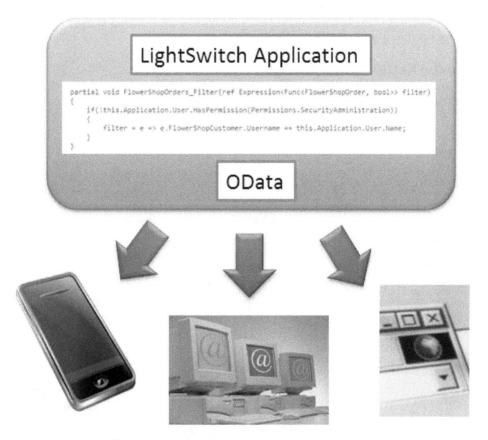

This allows you to centralize your business rules and security and have them enforced consistently no matter what client (web page, mobile phone, IPad) is accessing it.

You will not need to duplicate the business rules and security in each client that consumes your application. Each client will be simpler to create, and easier to maintain.

Chapter 2: Consuming OData in LightSwitch

Consuming OData in Visual Studio LightSwitch in Visual Studio 2012 (or higher) is very easy. When you consume an OData service in LightSwitch, its entities that you import behave like any other LightSwitch data source (such as internal entities, external SQL tables, and WCF RIA Services). This allows you to easily create mash-ups where you combine different data sources to create an application.

In this example, we will create an application that allows us to add our own reviews to the movies in the Netflix.com catalog. To do this, we will consume the Netflix OData service in our LightSwitch application. You can get information about the Netflix OData service at this link: http://developer.netflix.com/docs/oData_Catalog.

Connect To the Netflix OData Service

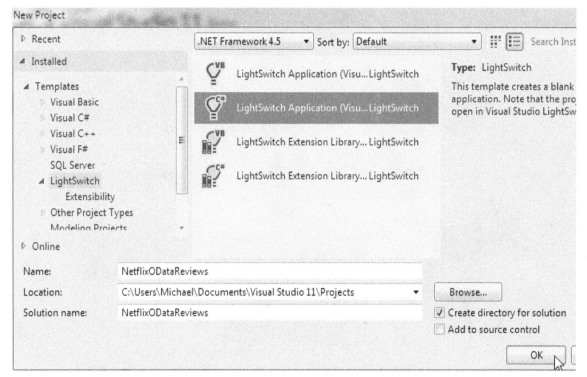

First, we create a new LightSwitch project.

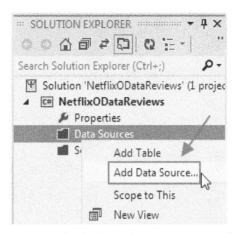

Next, we *right-click* on **Data Sources** in the **Solution Explorer**, and select **Add Data Source**.

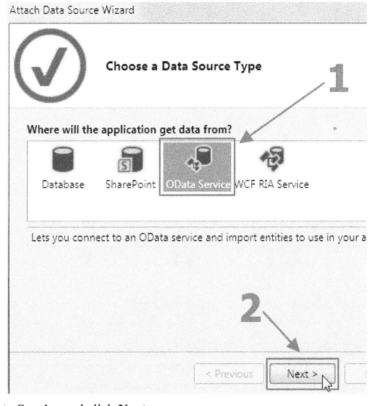

We select **OData Service** and click **Next**.

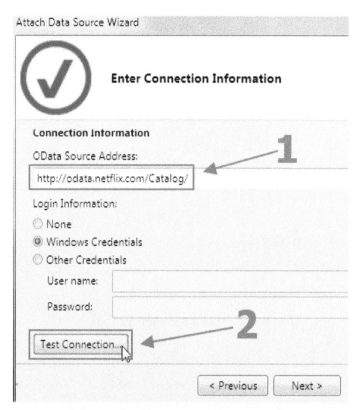

We enter the URL to the Netflix OData service and click the **Test Connection** button.

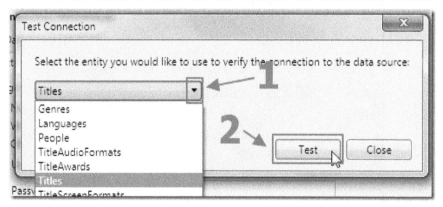

The **Test Connection** box will show, and ask us to select an entity to test.

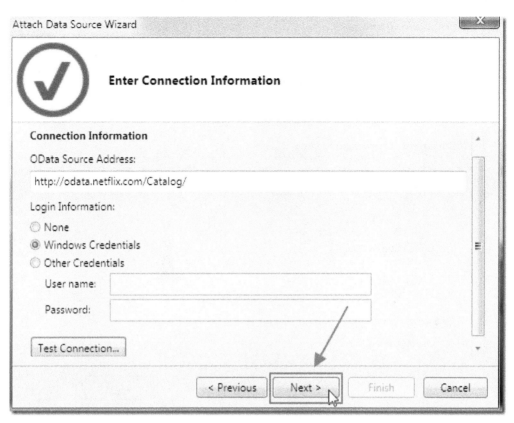

After testing, we return to the **Attach Data Source Wizard** and select **Next**.

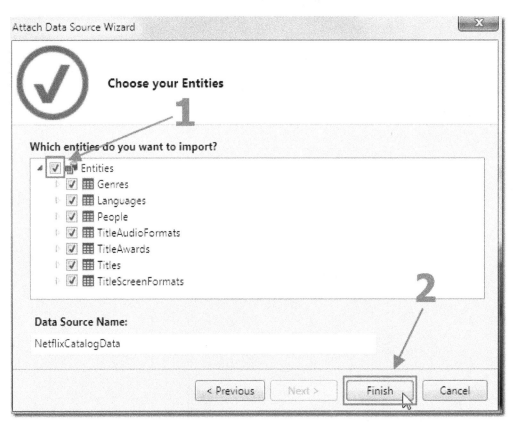

We select all the entities and click **Finish**.

We will receive warnings, but clicking **Continue** will import the entities.

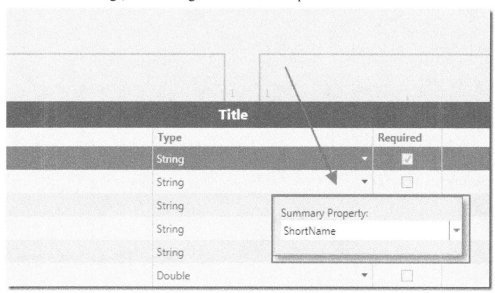

We open the **Title** entity, and in its **Properties**, set the **Summary Property** to the **ShortName** column.

Create the Screen

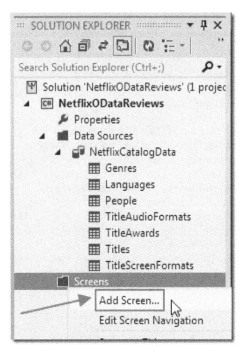

Now, we *right-click* on the **Screens** folder in the **Solution Explorer**, and select **Add Screen**.

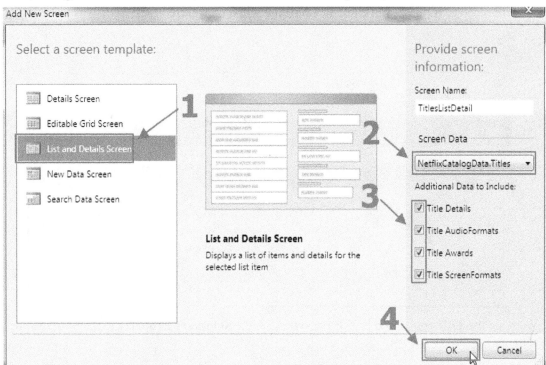

We create a **List and Details Screen**.

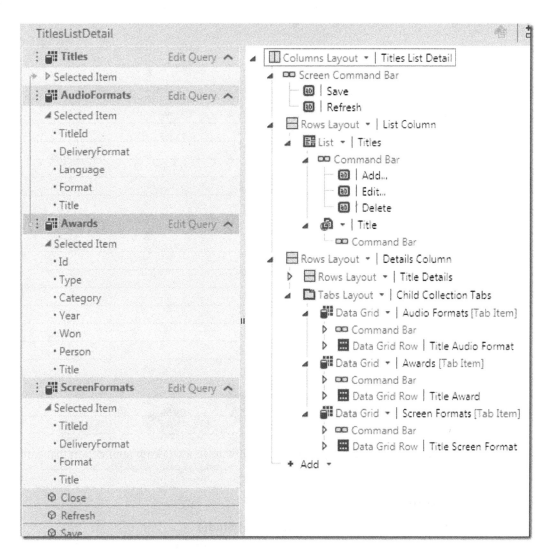

The screen will show in the designer.

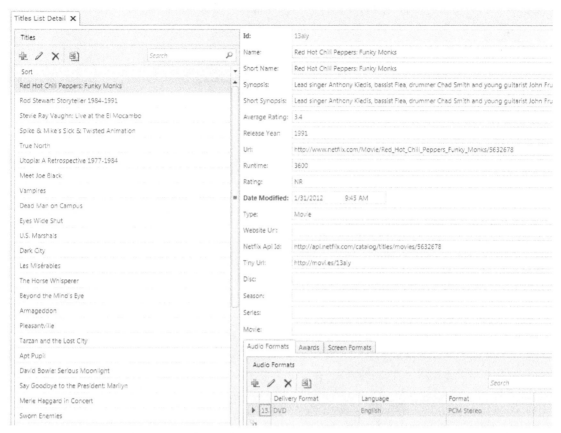

Now we press the **F5** key to run the application. We now have a working application that can browse the Netflix catalog.

Create the Mash-up

We close the running application, and return to **Visual Studio**.

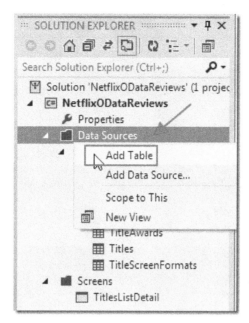

We now add a new Table (Entity).

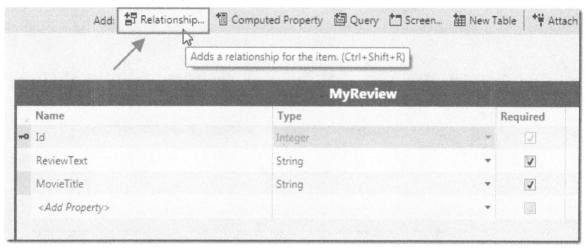

We create a table called **MyReview** with two fields:

- **ReviewText** – To hold the text of our review of the movie. We clear the **Maximum Length** field in the **Properties** for this field to allow for a long review.

- **MovieTitle** – To hold the title of the movie.

We then click the **Relationship** button.

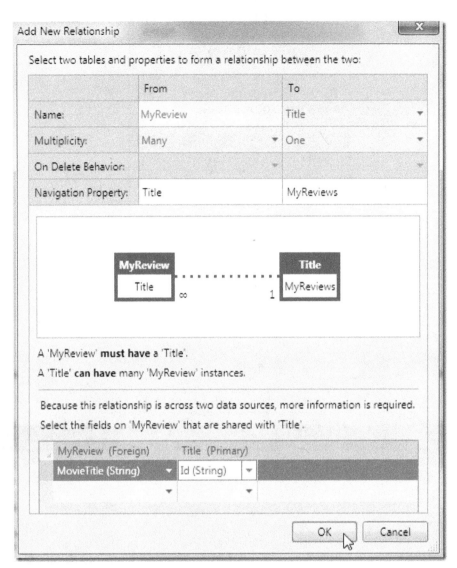

We create the relationship (for more information on creating relationships in LightSwitch, see: **How to: Define Data Relationships**: http://msdn.microsoft.com/en-us/library/ff852044.aspx).

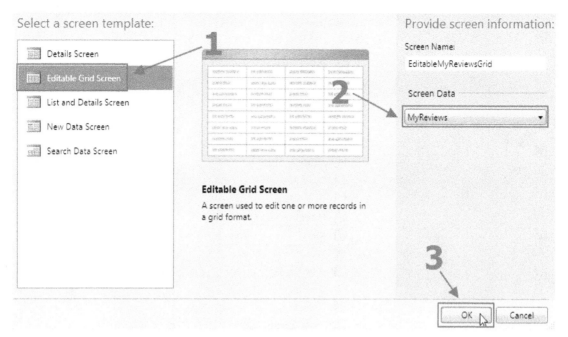

We then create an **Editable Grid Screen** for the table.

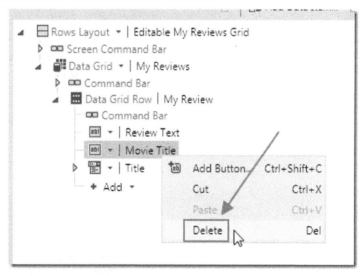

We remove **Movie Title** (the title will be shown in the **Title** field).

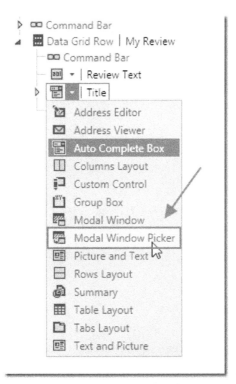

We change the control for the **Title** field to a **Modal Window Picker** (because it will allow us to easily choose a movie from the large list of movies. The default **Auto Complete Box** would attempt to load all the movies (over 1000 movies) in a single drop down).

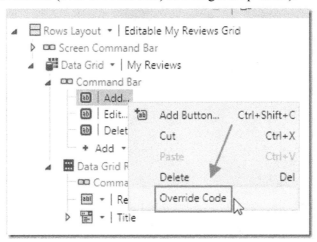

We *right-click* on the **Add** button, and select **Override Code**. We do this to prevent the automatic popup from opening (because that popup would try to show all the movies in the automatically created default drop down).

```
 LightSwitchApplication.EditableMyReviewsGrid
using System;
using System.Linq;
using System.IO;
using System.IO.IsolatedStorage;
using System.Collections.Generic;
using Microsoft.LightSwitch;
using Microsoft.LightSwitch.Framework.Client;
using Microsoft.LightSwitch.Presentation;
using Microsoft.LightSwitch.Presentation.Extensions;
namespace LightSwitchApplication
{
    public partial class EditableMyReviewsGrid
    {
        partial void gridAddAndEditNew_CanExecute(ref bool result)
        {
            // Write your code here.

        }

        partial void gridAddAndEditNew_Execute()
        {
            // Write your code here.
            MyReviews.AddNew();
        }
    }
}
```

We add the one line of code (in the red box in the previous image) to cause a blank row to be added to the grid when the button is pressed:

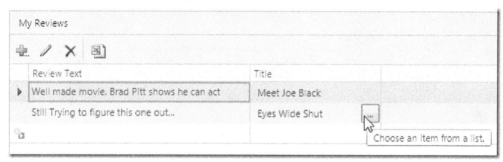

When we run the application we now have our mash-up!

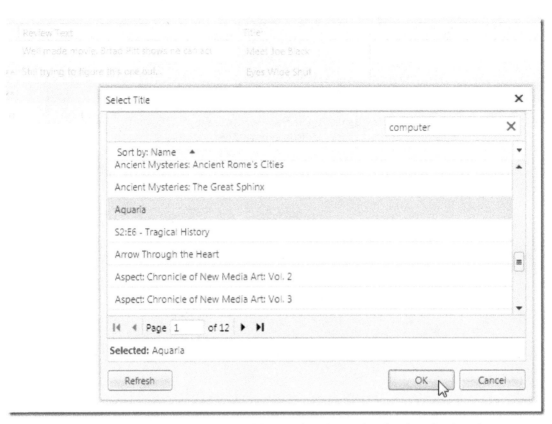

Notice that we now have a searchable, pageable, movie selector by simply selecting the **Modal Window Picker** for the **Title** field.

Chapter 3: Publishing OData in LightSwitch

The remainder of this book will cover scenarios associated with publishing OData in LightSwitch and consuming that OData in various clients including web pages and mobile applications.

Security is an important aspect to pay attention to. However, you will generally find that you can set security in the normal Silverlight client version of your LightSwitch application, and the OData security will always be the same. However, you must remember to look at each entity (table) and consider the security settings required.

Creating an entity, yet setting no security for it at all, will make that entity fully editable by any user. You would not want your Product entity to be updated by a user who has only a simple Customer account (they could change the price of the products!).

All of the remaining chapters and examples will use an order tracking application called **FlowerShop**, which is created for a fictitious florist.

The FlowerShop Application

(Note: The following code can be downloaded from the LightSwitchHelpWebsite.com download page at the link titled: *Accessing Your Visual Studio 2011 LightSwitch Application Using OData*)

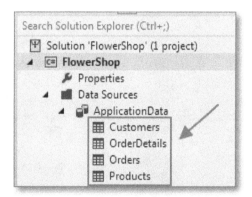

We create a new LightSwitch application, and we create four entities using the following schema and relationships (the following diagram was created by publishing the application and then using SQL Enterprise Manager to make the diagram):

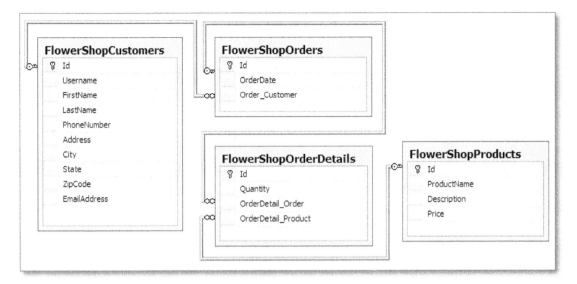

We create a **Products** screen:

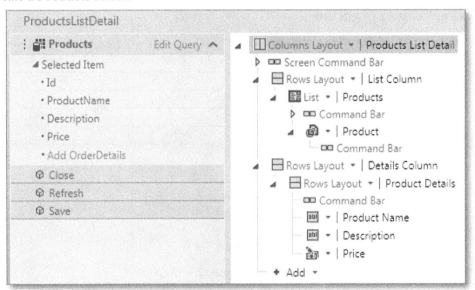

That allows **Products** to be entered when we run the program:

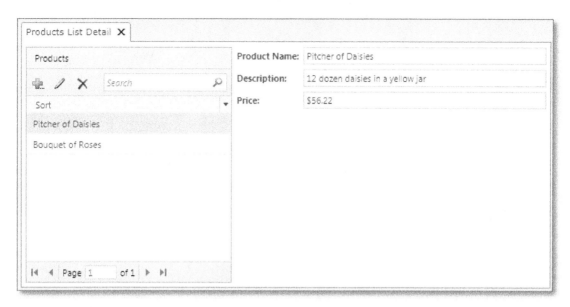

We create a **Customers** screen:

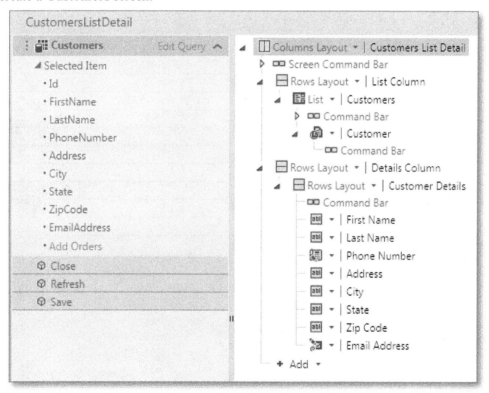

When the program is running it allows **Customers** to be entered:

We also create an **Orders** screen:

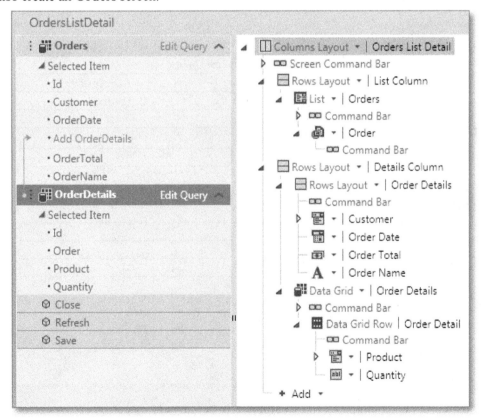

When the program is running, **Orders** as well as **Order Details** can be entered:

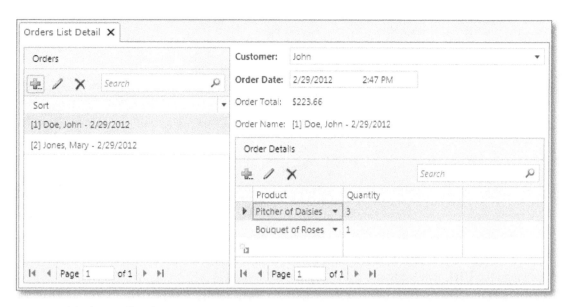

We **Publish** the application:

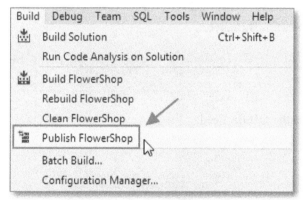

*Note: see **Deploying LightSwitch Applications** http://msdn.microsoft.com/en-us/library/ff872288(v=vs.110).aspx for instructions on publishing your LightSwitch application. You also have the option to simply run your LightSwitch application in debug mode; however, this runs the application with an address that uses a port number that constantly changes.*

We enter sample data:

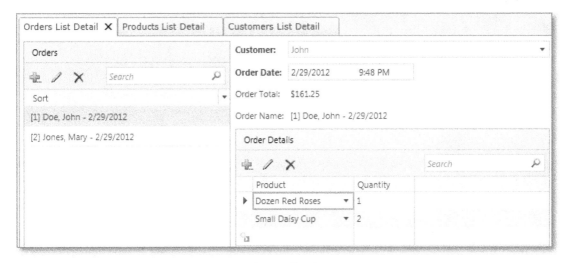

We change the **URL** that we use to get to the application …

… to a URL with **ApplicationData.svc**.

This will allow us to see the **OData** Feed.

```xml
<?xml version="1.0" encoding="UTF-8"?>
<service xmlns="http://www.w3.org/2007/app" xmlns:atom="http://www.w3.org/2005/Atom"
xml:base="http://localhost/FlowerShop/ApplicationData.svc/">
  <workspace>
    <atom:title>Default</atom:title>
    <collection href="Customers">
      <atom:title>Customers</atom:title>
    </collection>
    <collection href="Products">
      <atom:title>Products</atom:title>
    </collection>
    <collection href="Orders">
      <atom:title>Orders</atom:title>
    </collection>
    <collection href="OrderDetails">
      <atom:title>OrderDetails</atom:title>
    </collection>
  </workspace>
</service>
```

Using LinqPad

We can download and install **LinqPad** from: http://www.linqpad.net/. We add a connection:

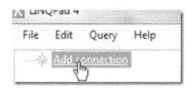

We select **WCF Data Services (OData)** and click **Next**.

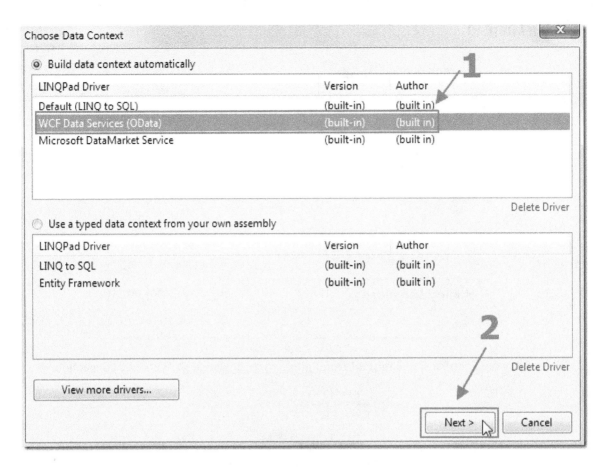

We enter the **URL** to our LightSwitch application and click **OK**.

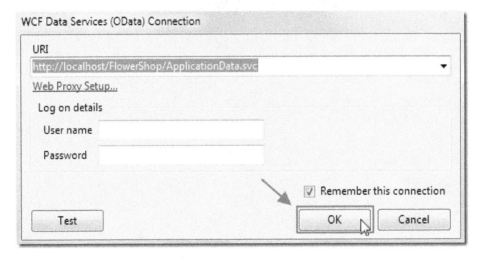

The **Entities** will show.

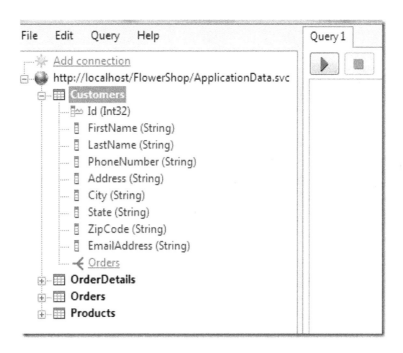

We can now use the following query (in C# Statement(s) mode):

```
var DozenRedRoses =
from Product in Products
where Product.ProductName == "Dozen Red Roses"
select Product;
DozenRedRoses.Dump("The Dozen Red Roses");
// Set Product ID
var intProductID = DozenRedRoses.FirstOrDefault().Id;
var OrderDetailsForRoses =
from OrderDetail in OrderDetails
where OrderDetail.Product.Id == intProductID
where OrderDetail.Quantity > 1
select OrderDetail;
OrderDetailsForRoses.Dump("The order details for more than 2 roses");
// Get Order Detail IDs
List<int> OrderDetailIDs = new List<int>();
foreach (var element in OrderDetailsForRoses)
{
        OrderDetailIDs.Add(element.OrderDetail_Order);
}
foreach (var element in OrderDetailIDs)
{
        var OrderForRoses =
        from Order in Orders
        where Order.Id == element
        select Order;

        OrderForRoses.Dump("A order for more than 2 Red Roses");
}
```

To produce the following result:

The Dozen Red Roses

▲ IOrderedQueryable<Product> (1 item)

Id	ProductName	Description	Price	OrderDetails
1	Dozen Red Roses	12 long stem red roses	75.25	Collection<OrderDetail> (0 items)

The order details for more than 2 roses

▲ IOrderedQueryable<OrderDetail> (1 item)

Id	Quantity	OrderDetail_Order	OrderDetail_Product	Order	Product
4	2	2	1	null	null

A order for more than 2 Red Roses

▲ IOrderedQueryable<Order> (1 item)

Id	OrderDate	Order_Customer	Customer	OrderDetails
2	2/29/2012 9:49:25 PM	2	null	Collection<OrderDetail> (0 items)

Security

The LightSwitch **OData** service points provide full security. For example, we can open **Properties** in the LightSwitch application, and enable **Forms Authentication**.

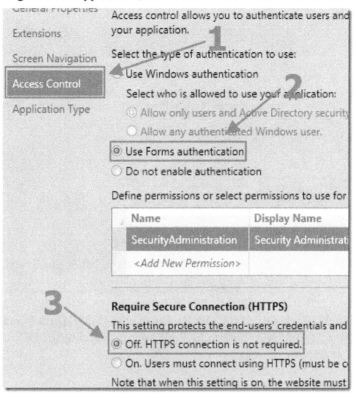

When we deploy the application again and navigate to the **OData** service points, it now prompts us for a valid account (the account is any normal user account for the LightSwitch application).

The Microsoft article, **Accessing Data Service Resources (WCF Data Services)** (http://msdn.microsoft.com/en-us/library/dd728283.aspx), explains the **OData** syntax and provides a lot of examples:

System Query Options

OData defines a set of system query options that you can use to perform traditional query operations against reso example, the following URI returns the set of all the `Order` entities, along with related `Order_Detail` entities, th

```
http://services.odata.org/Northwind/Northwind.svc/Orders?$filter=not endswith(ShipPosta
erby=ShipCity
```

The entries in the returned feed are also ordered by the value of the ShipCity property of the orders.

WCF Data Services supports the following OData system query options:

Query Option	Description
$orderby	Defines a default sort order for entities in the returned feed. The following query orders the return `http://services.odata.org/Northwind/Northwind.svc/Customers?$orderby=Cou` For more information, see OData: OrderBy System Query Option ($orderby).
$top	Specifies the number of entities to include in the returned feed. The following example skips the f `http://services.odata.org/Northwind/Northwind.svc/Customers?$skip=10&$t` For more information, see OData: Top System Query Option ($top).
$skip	Specifies the number of entities to skip before starting to return entities in the feed. The following

However, you will find it much easier to implement **OData** using **OData** client libraries such as the libraries described in the reminder of this book.

Chapter 4: Reading OData Using Server Side Code

In this chapter we will cover creating ASP.NET pages that we can connect to LightSwitch using OData. There are many ways to call LightSwitch OData collections. This chapter will demonstrate methods that use server side code.

This chapter will only cover reading OData, the next chapter will cover updating, deleting and inserting data.

We will add .aspx pages to the LightSwitch project. This will make deployment, especially to Windows Azure (http://www.windowsazure.com), easier. You can use the exact same code and methods to create pages in a separate stand-alone project.

The important concepts to learn from this chapter are creating a service reference, and passing the forms authentication cookie to the LightSwitch OData service.

We will start by looking at the finished application...

(Note: The following code can be downloaded from the LightSwitchHelpWebsite.com download page at the link titled: *Calling LightSwitch 2011 OData Using Server Side Code*)

The Application

When we log into the sample application, we see that it is a standard order entry application.

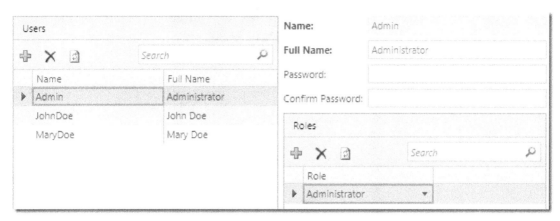

We have one administrator (Admin) and two non-administrator users (JohnDoe, MaryDoe).

If we navigate to the **Login.aspx** page, we see a web application that is optimized for mobile displays. We log in using the normal LightSwitch username and password for each account.

A normal user will see only their orders.

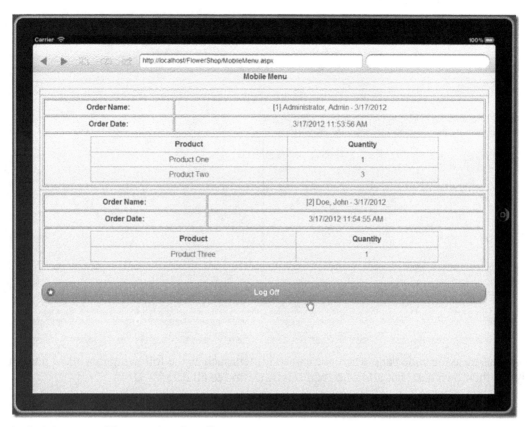

An Administrator will see orders for all users.

Set-Up and Security

When we expose our LightSwitch application entities over **OData**, we must set security.

For example, to set security on the **Order** entity, we select the **Write Code** menu, and then the **_Filter** method.

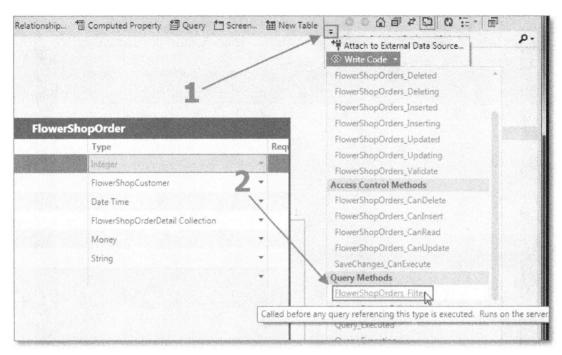

This takes us to the code page where we can add filters such as the following that allow a user to only see their own data, but allow an **Administrator** to see all data:

```
public partial class ApplicationDataService
{

    // Filters

    partial void FlowerShopCustomers_Filter(ref Expression<Func<FlowerShopCustomer, bool>> filter)
    {
        if(!this.Application.User.HasPermission(Permissions.SecurityAdministration))
        {
            filter = e => e.Username == this.Application.User.Name;
        }
    }

    partial void FlowerShopOrderDetails_Filter(ref Expression<Func<FlowerShopOrderDetail, bool>> filter)
    {
        if(!this.Application.User.HasPermission(Permissions.SecurityAdministration))
        {
            filter = e => e.FlowerShopOrder.FlowerShopCustomer.Username == this.Application.User.Name;
        }
    }

    partial void FlowerShopOrders_Filter(ref Expression<Func<FlowerShopOrder, bool>> filter)
    {
        if(!this.Application.User.HasPermission(Permissions.SecurityAdministration))
        {
            filter = e => e.FlowerShopCustomer.Username == this.Application.User.Name;
        }
    }

    // Updating
```

If the current user has the **SecurityAdministration** permission (this is the standard permission that all administrators have), the results are not filtered. If they do not have the **SecurityAdministration** permission, the results from each entity are filtered to only show the records that are associated with the current user.

We also go into **Settings** and ensure we have **Forms authentication** enabled.

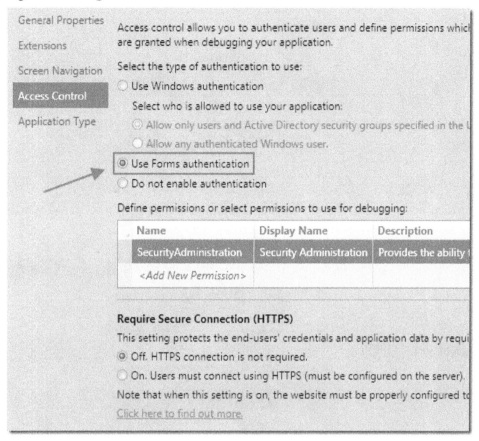

(you can use other authentication methods, but the code in this example will only work with **Forms authentication**)

Set-Up – OData Reference

When using server side code to access OData you will need to create a service reference to the OData service point.

We now need to create a **service reference** to the LightSwitch **OData** service. To do this, we switch to **File View** in **Visual Studio**.

We select **Show All Files**.

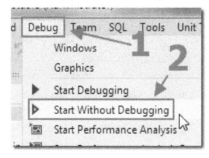

Next, we select **Start Without Debugging**.

The web browser will open, and we will see a **URL**.

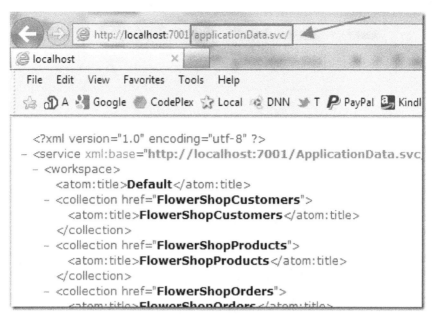

We alter the **URL** to point the **URL** to **applicationData.svc**, and copy the entire **URL** (you may have to turn off *Feed Reading View* in **Internet Explorer** to see the collections in the web browser).

The URL will contain a port number. This port number changes each time we run the application in debug mode. However, we will add code in a later step that will dynamically set the web address so it will always be set to the correct address that is the current address for the application.

Note: applicationData.svc will only show entities that are contained in the default internal intrinsic LightSwitch database. If we connect to external data sources (including custom WCF RIA Services) we would access them using a .svc OData service that matches the name of the external data source. See chapter 8 for an example.

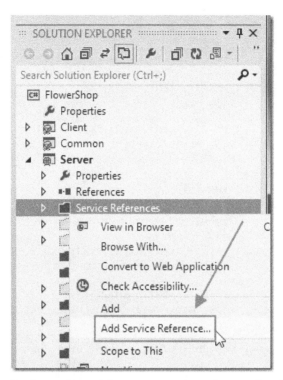

We return to **Visual Studio** (keep the web browser open), and we *right-click* on **Server/Service References**, and select **Add Service Reference**.

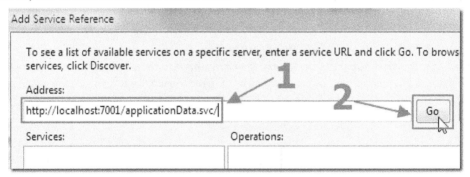

We paste in the **URL** that we copied in the **Address** box, and we click the **Go** button.

Note: The web address (URL) above contains the port number; however, at this time we only need to connect to the service to create the proxy class. We will add code that will set the actual web address dynamically.

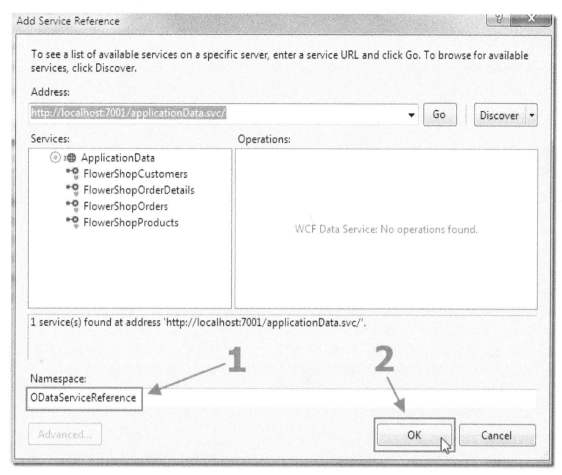

After the collections show, we change the namespace to **ODataServiceReference** and click **OK**.

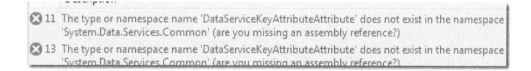

If we try to build the project it may no longer build.

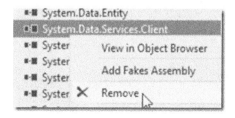

We have to remove the **System.Data.Services.Client** assembly reference from the **Server** project to fix the problem.

Set-Up – LightSwitch OData Forms Authentication Security

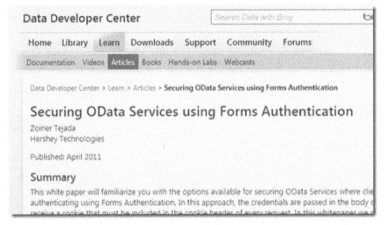

Now, we follow the **Forms Authentication Configuration** directions in the article: Securing OData Services using Forms Authentication (http://msdn.microsoft.com/en-us/data/gg192996).

We add a partial class that will get the authentication cookie that is created when the user logs in, and we will use it to set an authentication cookie that we will attach to each **OData** call:

```
partial void OnContextCreated()
{
    this.SendingRequest +=
        new EventHandler<SendingRequestEventArgs>(OnSendingRequest);
}
void OnSendingRequest(object sender, SendingRequestEventArgs e)
{
    // Get the Forms auth cookie
    var AuthCookie = HttpContext.Current.Request.Cookies[FormsAuthentication.FormsCookieName];
    if (AuthCookie != null)
    {
        Cookie objCookie = new Cookie();
        objCookie.Domain = HttpContext.Current.Request.Url.DnsSafeHost;
        objCookie.Expires = AuthCookie.Expires;
        objCookie.HttpOnly = AuthCookie.HttpOnly;
        objCookie.Name = AuthCookie.Name;
        objCookie.Path = AuthCookie.Path;
        objCookie.Secure = AuthCookie.Secure;
        objCookie.Value = AuthCookie.Value;
        ((HttpWebRequest)e.Request).CookieContainer = new CookieContainer();
        ((HttpWebRequest)e.Request).CookieContainer.Add(objCookie);
    }
}
```

The following code is used to determine the current base address of the LightSwitch application so that the **URL** to the **OData** service will be dynamically set to the correct address:

```
public static string BaseSiteUrl
{
    get
    {
        HttpContext context = HttpContext.Current;
        string baseUrl =
            context.Request.Url.Scheme
            + "://"
            + context.Request.Url.Authority
            + context.Request.ApplicationPath.TrimEnd('/') + '/';
        return baseUrl;
    }
}
```

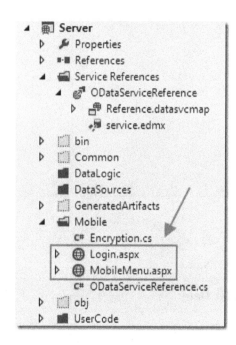

We also add a **Login.aspx** and a **MobileMenu.aspx** page. In the **Login** page, we use the following code:

```csharp
public partial class Login : System.Web.UI.Page
{
    protected void Page_Load(object sender, EventArgs e)
    {
        // When a user first comes to this page log them out
        if (!Page.IsPostBack)
        {
            FormsAuthentication.SignOut();
        }
    }
    protected void ctrlLogin_Authenticate(object sender, AuthenticateEventArgs e)
    {
        if (Membership.ValidateUser(ctrlLogin.UserName, ctrlLogin.Password))
        {
            // Set the forms authentication cookie that will be used in the OData requests
            FormsAuthentication.SetAuthCookie(ctrlLogin.UserName, false);
            e.Authenticated = true;
            Response.Redirect("~/MobileMenu.aspx");
        }
        else
        {
            e.Authenticated = false;
            lblMessage.Text = "Login failed";
        }
    }
}
```

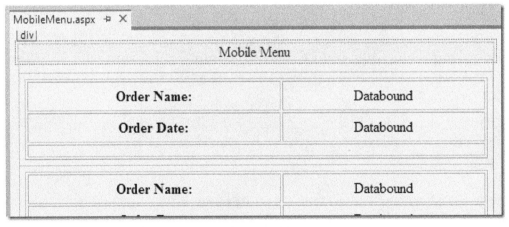

We use the following code for the markup of the **MobileMenu.aspx** page:

```
<div data-role="page">
    <div data-role="header" align="center" data-theme="c">
        Mobile Menu
    </div>
    <!-- /header -->
    <div data-role="content">
        <asp:gridview id="gvOrders" runat="server" autogeneratecolumns="False">
            <Columns>
                <asp:TemplateField HeaderText=" ">
                    <ItemTemplate>
                        <table align="center" border="1">
                            <tr>
                                <td><strong>Order Name:</strong></td>
                                <td>
                                    <asp:Label runat="server" Text='<%# Eval("OrderName") %>' />
                                </td>
                            </tr>
                            <tr>
                                <td>
                                    <strong>Order Date:</strong></td>
                                <td>
                                    <asp:Label runat="server" Text='<%# Eval("OrderDate") %>' />
                                </td>
                            </tr>
                            <tr>
                                <td colspan="2" style="text-align: center">
                                    <asp:GridView ID="gvOrderDetails" runat="server" autogeneratecolumns="False"
                                        DataSource='<%# Eval("OrderDetailsInfo") %>' align="center" Width="80%">
                                        <Columns>
                                            <asp:BoundField DataField="Product" HeaderText="Product" />
                                            <asp:BoundField DataField="Quantity" HeaderText="Quantity">
                                                <ItemStyle HorizontalAlign="Center" />
                                            </asp:BoundField>
                                        </Columns>
                                    </asp:GridView>
                                </td>
                            </tr>
                        </table>
                    </ItemTemplate>
                </asp:TemplateField>
            </Columns>
        </asp:gridview>
        <br />
        <asp:hyperlink id="lnkLogOff" runat="server" navigateurl="~/Login.aspx" data-role="button"
            data-ajax="false" data-icon="star" data-theme="b" text="Log Off" />
    </div>
```

The following code is used to display the **Orders**:

```
private void ShowOrders()
{
    // Create DataContext
    ODataServiceReference.ApplicationData objApplicationData =
        new ODataServiceReference.ApplicationData(new Uri(string.Format(@"{0}applicationdata.svc/", BaseSiteUrl)));
    // Query OData source
    var result = from FlowerShopOrders in objApplicationData.FlowerShopOrders
                    .Expand(x => x.FlowerShopCustomer)
                    .Expand(x => x.FlowerShopOrderDetail)
                select FlowerShopOrders;
    // Collection to hold Orders
    List<OrderInfo> colOrderInfo = new List<OrderInfo>();
    // Loop thru orders
    foreach (var item in result)
    {
        // Create new Order
        OrderInfo objOrderInfo = new OrderInfo();
        objOrderInfo.OrderID = item.Id;
        objOrderInfo.OrderName =
            String.Format("[{0}] {1}, {2} - {3}",
            item.Id,
            item.FlowerShopCustomer.LastName,
            item.FlowerShopCustomer.FirstName,
            item.OrderDate.ToShortDateString());
        objOrderInfo.OrderDate = item.OrderDate;
        // Collection to hold Order Details
        objOrderInfo.OrderDetailsInfo = new List<OrderDetailsInfo>();
        // Loop thru order details
        foreach (var OrderDetail in item.FlowerShopOrderDetail)
        {
            // Create new Order Detail
            OrderDetailsInfo objOrderDetailsInfo = new OrderDetailsInfo();
            // Create a new DataContext
            ODataServiceReference.ApplicationData objApplicationData2 =
                new ODataServiceReference.ApplicationData(new Uri(string.Format(@"{0}applicationdata.svc/", BaseSiteUrl)));
            // Query OData source
            var objOrderDetails = (from OrderDetails in objApplicationData2.FlowerShopOrderDetails
                                    .Expand(x => x.FlowerShopProduct)
                                where OrderDetails.Id == OrderDetail.Id
                                select OrderDetails).FirstOrDefault();
            objOrderDetailsInfo.Id = OrderDetail.Id;
            objOrderDetailsInfo.Product = objOrderDetails.FlowerShopProduct.ProductName;
            objOrderDetailsInfo.Quantity = OrderDetail.Quantity;
            // Add Order Detail
            objOrderInfo.OrderDetailsInfo.Add(objOrderDetailsInfo);
        }
        // Add Order
        colOrderInfo.Add(objOrderInfo);
    }
    // Bind entire colection to GridView
    gvOrders.DataSource = colOrderInfo;
    gvOrders.DataBind();
}
```

There is also an **OrderInfo** class used to display the orders:

```
#region OrderInfo
public class OrderInfo
{
    int _OrderID;
    public int OrderID
    {
        get { return _OrderID; }
        set { _OrderID = value; }
    }
    string _OrderName;
    public string OrderName
    {
        get { return _OrderName; }
        set { _OrderName = value; }
    }
    DateTime _OrderDate;
    public DateTime OrderDate
    {
        get { return _OrderDate; }
        set { _OrderDate = value; }
    }
    string _HyperLink;
    public string HyperLink
    {
        get { return _HyperLink; }
        set { _HyperLink = value; }
    }
}
#endregion
```

There is also an **OrderDetailsInfo** class used to display the order details:

```csharp
#region OrderDetailsInfo
public class OrderDetailsInfo
{
    int _Id;
    public int Id
    {
        get { return _Id; }
        set { _Id = value; }
    }

    string _Product;
    public string Product
    {
        get { return _Product; }
        set { _Product = value; }
    }

    int _Quantity;
    public int Quantity
    {
        get { return _Quantity; }
        set { _Quantity = value; }
    }
}
#endregion
```

Adding the .ASPX Pages to the Build

We now need to add the **Login.aspx** and **MobileMenu.aspx** pages to the build file, so that LightSwitch will include them in the build.

If we do not do this, the pages will not be present when you **debug** or **publish** the application.

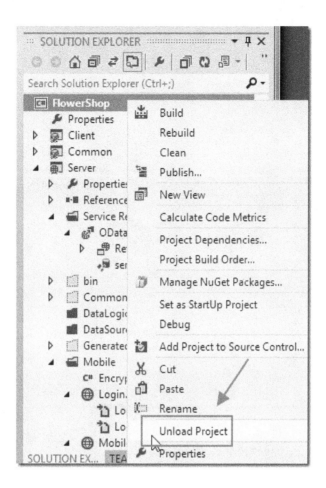

We switch to **File View**, *right-click* on the LightSwitch project, and select **Unload Project**.

Note: If Visual Studio throws an error or crashes, just close Visual Studio and then re-open the project.

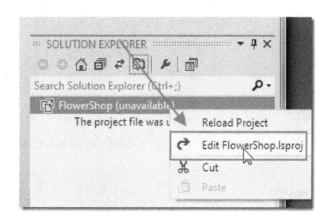

We *Right-click* on the unloaded project and select **Edit**.

```
180      </_BuildFile>
181      <_BuildFile Include="default.htm">
182          <SubFolder>
183          </SubFolder>
184          <PublishType>
185          </PublishType>
186      </_BuildFile>
187      <_BuildFile Include="Server\Mobile\Login.aspx">
188          <SubFolder>
189          </SubFolder>
190          <PublishType>
191          </PublishType>
192      </_BuildFile>
193      <_BuildFile Include="Server\Mobile\MobileMenu.aspx">
194          <SubFolder>
195          </SubFolder>
196          <PublishType>
197          </PublishType>
198      </_BuildFile>
199      </ItemGroup>
200      <ItemGroup>
201          <LightSwitchExtension Include="Microsoft.LightSwitch.Ex
```

We add the entries for the pages to the **_buildFile** section.

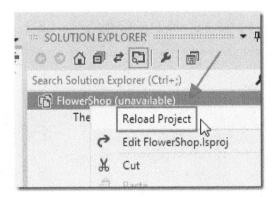

We then **Reload** the project. The project will now include the pages when you **debug** or **publish** the application.

Debugging Using 'Test User'

When you are debugging with LightSwitch, you are always a user named **TestUser**. You are also automatically logged in.

To log in as this user in the **Login.aspx** page, you will need the password. To establish a password, you will need to add a user named **TestUser** to the **Users** table in LightSwitch security:

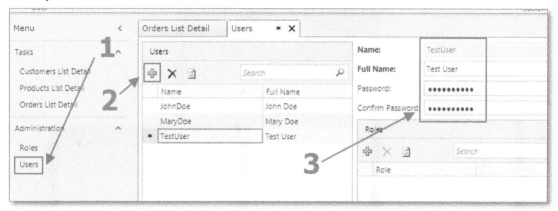

The password that you set is the password that you will enter into the **Login.aspx** page.

An Important Note about SSL

All the **OData** calls in this application contain the username and password sent in clear text. This is because this sample application is using Forms Security and the 'client' is a standard web page.

A production application must run on a webserver that has SSL enabled for all transactions. Otherwise, a hacker with a packet sniffer can easily get the usernames and passwords of your users who are connecting to your site using public Wi-Fi access points or other unsecure networks.

Chapter 5: A Full CRUD OData jQuery Mobile Application (Using Server Side Code)

In this chapter we will cover **Creating**, **Reading**, **Updating**, and **Deleting** (otherwise known as CRUD). We will also use **jQuery Mobile** (http://jQueryMobile.com), and target the sample application to work with mobile devices.

(Note: The following code can be downloaded from the LightSwitchHelpWebsite.com download page at the link titled: *A Full CRUD LightSwitch jQuery Mobile Application*)

The Application

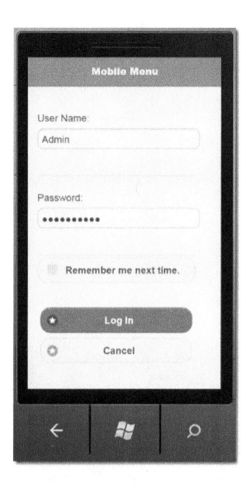

When the LightSwitch application runs, we navigate to the **MobileMenu.aspx** page, and we are presented with a login menu.

Note: If using Internet Explorer in "compatibility mode" the login won't work, so turn off "compatibility mode" in Internet Explorer when testing.

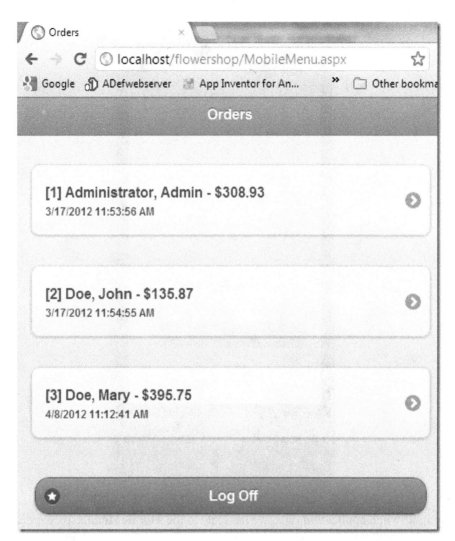

If a user is an Administrator, they will see all orders, otherwise they will only see (and be able to edit) their own orders.

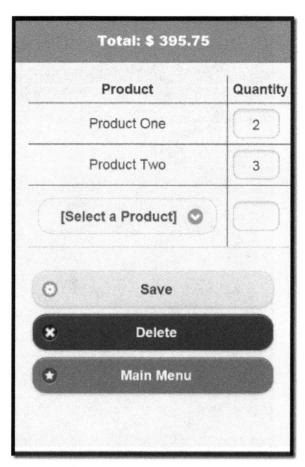

Clicking on an order displays the details. To remove an item, set the **Quantity** to 0, and click **Save**.

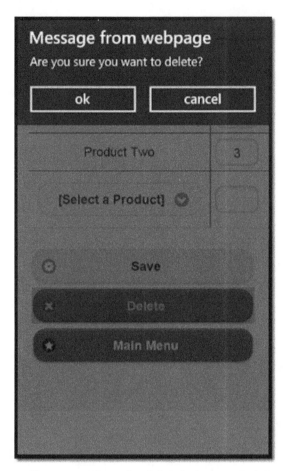

Clicking the **Delete** button allows an order to be deleted. A non-administrator will not be able to delete an order (this is by design).

Clicking on the dropdown at the bottom of the order details table allows you to choose a product to add.

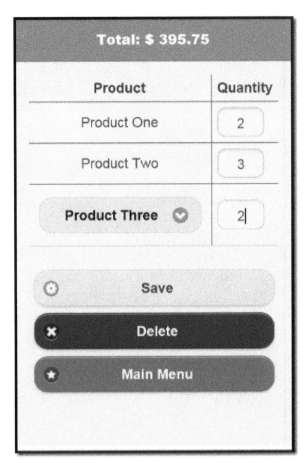

Entering a quantity and clicking **Save** adds the product to the order.

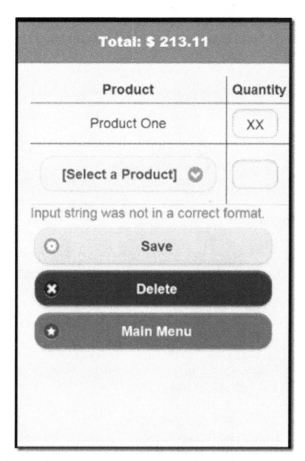

All the validation, including the messages, is generated by LightSwitch. For example, in the image above, an invalid quantity is entered for Product One (error codes are also returned if you need to implement more *user friendly* validation errors).

The Business Layer

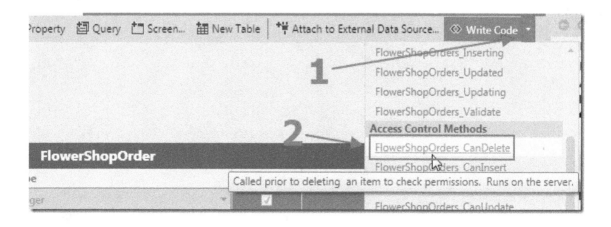

First, we implement the **_CanDelete** methods on the **FlowerShopOrders** and **FlowerShopOrderDetails** entities to prevent any non-administrator from deleting data:

```
partial void FlowerShopOrders_CanDelete(ref bool result)
{
    result = this.Application.User.HasPermission(Permissions.SecurityAdministration);
}
partial void FlowerShopOrderDetails_CanDelete(ref bool result)
{
    result = this.Application.User.HasPermission(Permissions.SecurityAdministration);
}
```

The ASP.NET Web Pages

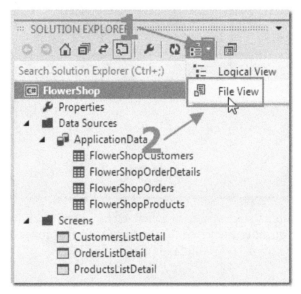

The majority of the application is in the **ASP.NET** web pages that we can access in the **File View**.

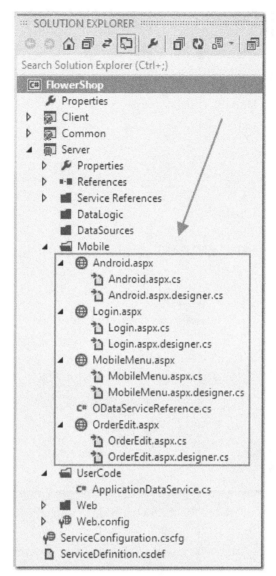

All the pages are contained in the **Server** / **Mobile** folder.

Note: The Android.aspx page is not used in this example, but is covered in the article: Communicating With LightSwitch Using Android App Inventor (http://lightswitchhelpwebsite.com/Blog/tabid/61/EntryId/125/Communicating-With-LightSwitch-Using-Android-App-Inventor.aspx).

The **OrderEdit.aspx** page was added for this chapter, and the existing **Login.aspx** page and **MobileMenu.aspx** page (from the previous chapter) were altered for this chapter.

The Login Page

The **Login.aspx** page was altered to the following code to implement the **jQuery Mobile** framework that optimizes the page for mobile devices:

```
<%@ Page Language="C#" AutoEventWireup="true" CodeBehind="Login.aspx.cs" Inherits="LightSwitchApplication.Login" %>
<!DOCTYPE html>
<html>
<head id="Head1" runat="server">
    <title>Mobile Login</title>
    <meta name="viewport" content="width=device-width, initial-scale=1">
    <link rel="stylesheet" href="http://code.jquery.com/mobile/1.0.1/jquery.mobile-1.0.1.min.css" />
    <script src="http://code.jquery.com/jquery-1.6.4.min.js"></script>
    <script src="http://code.jquery.com/mobile/1.0.1/jquery.mobile-1.0.1.min.js"></script>
</head>
```

The following shows the markup for the main layout template:

```
<LayoutTemplate>
    <table border="0" cellpadding="1" cellspacing="0"
        style="border-collapse:collapse;" width="100%">
        <tr>
            <td>
                <table border="0" cellpadding="0" width="100%">
                    <tr>
                        <td data-role="fieldcontain">
                            <asp:Label ID="UserNameLabel" runat="server"
                                AssociatedControlID="UserName">User Name:</asp:Label>
                            <asp:TextBox ID="UserName" runat="server"></asp:TextBox>
                            <asp:RequiredFieldValidator ID="UserNameRequired" runat="server"
                                ControlToValidate="UserName" ErrorMessage="User Name is required."
                                ToolTip="User Name is required."
                                ValidationGroup="MainLogin">*</asp:RequiredFieldValidator>
                        </td>
                    </tr>
                    <tr>
                        <td data-role="fieldcontain">
                            <asp:Label ID="PasswordLabel" runat="server"
                                AssociatedControlID="Password">Password:</asp:Label>
                            <asp:TextBox ID="Password" runat="server" TextMode="Password"></asp:TextBox>
                            <asp:RequiredFieldValidator ID="PasswordRequired" runat="server"
                                ControlToValidate="Password" ErrorMessage="Password is required."
                                ToolTip="Password is required."
                                ValidationGroup="MainLogin">*</asp:RequiredFieldValidator>
                        </td>
                    </tr>
                    <tr>
                        <td>
                            <asp:CheckBox ID="RememberMe" runat="server" Text="Remember me next time." />
                        </td>
                    </tr>
                    <tr>
                        <td align="left" style="color:Red;">
                            <asp:Literal ID="FailureText" runat="server" EnableViewState="False"></asp:Literal>
                        </td>
                    </tr>
                    <tr>
                        <td align="left" data-role="fieldcontain">
                            <asp:Button ID="LoginButton" runat="server" CommandName="Login" Text="Log In"
                                ValidationGroup="MainLogin" data-ajax="false" data-icon="star" data-theme="b" />
                            <a data-ajax="false" data-icon="star" data-role="button" href="MobileMenu.aspx">
                                Cancel</a> </td>
                    </tr>
                    <tr>
                        <td align="left">
                             </td>
                    </tr>
                </table>
            </td>
        </tr>
    </table>
</LayoutTemplate>
```

The following is the code behind in **Login.aspx.cs** page:

```
using System;
using System.Collections.Generic;
using System.Linq;
using System.Net;
using System.Web;
using System.Web.Security;
using System.Web.UI;
using System.Web.UI.WebControls;
namespace LightSwitchApplication
{
    public partial class Login : System.Web.UI.Page
    {
        protected void Page_Load(object sender, EventArgs e)
        {
            // When a user first comes to this page log them out
            if (this.Request.QueryString["logoff"] != null)
            {
                if (this.Request.QueryString["logoff"] == "true")
                {
                    FormsAuthentication.SignOut();
                }
            }
        }
        protected void ctrlLogin_Authenticate(object sender, AuthenticateEventArgs e)
        {
            if (Membership.ValidateUser(ctrlLogin.UserName, ctrlLogin.Password))
            {
                // Set the forms authentication cookie that will be used in the OData requests
                FormsAuthentication.SetAuthCookie(ctrlLogin.UserName, true);
                e.Authenticated = true;
                Response.Redirect("~/MobileMenu.aspx");
            }
            else
            {
                e.Authenticated = false;
                ctrlLogin.FailureText = "Login failed";
            }
        }
    }
}
```

Mobile Menu Page

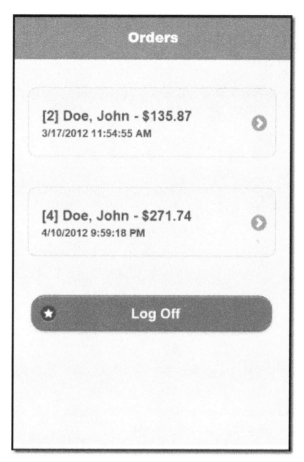

The **MobileMenu.aspx** page has been altered to the following code:

```
<%@ Page Language="C#" AutoEventWireup="true" CodeBehind="MobileMenu.aspx.cs"
    Inherits="LightSwitchApplication.Mobile.MobileMenu" %>
<!DOCTYPE html>
<html>
        <head>
    <title>Orders</title>
        <meta charset="utf-8">
        <meta name="viewport" content="width=device-width, initial-scale=1">
    <link rel="stylesheet" href="http://code.jquery.com/mobile/1.0.1/jquery.mobile-1.0.1.min.css" />
    <script src="http://code.jquery.com/jquery-1.6.4.min.js"></script>
    <script src="http://code.jquery.com/mobile/1.0.1/jquery.mobile-1.0.1.min.js"></script>
</head>
<body>
    <form id="form1" runat="server">
    <div data-role="page" class="type-interior">
        <div data-role="header" data-theme="b">
            <h1>Orders</h1>
        </div>
        <!-- /header -->
            <div data-role="content">
                <asp:datalist class="content-primary" id="gvOrders" style="width: 100%" runat="server">
                    <ItemTemplate>
                    <ul data-role="listview" data-inset="true" data-theme="c">
                                <li><a data-ajax="false" href='<%# Eval("HyperLink") %>'>
                                    <h3><asp:Label runat="server" Text='<%# Eval("OrderName") %>' /></h3>
                                    <p><strong><asp:Label runat="server" Text='<%# Eval("OrderDate") %>' /></strong></p>
                                </a></li>
                    </ul>
                    </ItemTemplate>
                </asp:datalist>
                <br />
                    <asp:hyperlink id="lnkLogOff" runat="server" navigateurl="~/Login.aspx?logoff=true"
                        data-role="button" data-ajax="false" data-icon="star" data-theme="b" text="Log Off" />
            </div>
            <!-- /content -->
        </div>
        <!-- /page -->
    </form>
</body>
</html>
```

The **MobileMenu.aspx.cs** page was also altered. The following code shows the imports, **BaseSiteUrl** property, and the **Page_Load** method:

```
using System;
using System.Collections.Generic;
using System.Linq;
using System.Net;
using System.Web;
using System.Web.Security;
using System.Web.UI;
using System.Web.UI.WebControls;
using Microsoft.VisualBasic;
namespace LightSwitchApplication.Mobile
{
    public partial class MobileMenu : System.Web.UI.Page
    {
        #region BaseSiteUrl
        public static string BaseSiteUrl
        {
            get
            {
                HttpContext context = HttpContext.Current;
                string baseUrl = context.Request.Url.Scheme
                    + "://"
                    + context.Request.Url.Authority
                    + context.Request.ApplicationPath.TrimEnd('/') + '/';
                return baseUrl;
            }
        }
        #endregion
        protected void Page_Load(object sender, EventArgs e)
        {
            if (User.Identity.IsAuthenticated) // Logged in
            {
                ShowOrders();
            }
            else // Not Logged In
            {
                Response.Redirect("~/Login.aspx");
            }
        }
    }
```

There is an **OrderInfo** class used to display the orders:

```csharp
#region OrderInfo
public class OrderInfo
{
    int _OrderID;
    public int OrderID
    {
        get { return _OrderID; }
        set { _OrderID = value; }
    }
    string _OrderName;
    public string OrderName
    {
        get { return _OrderName; }
        set { _OrderName = value; }
    }
    DateTime _OrderDate;
    public DateTime OrderDate
    {
        get { return _OrderDate; }
        set { _OrderDate = value; }
    }
    string _HyperLink;
    public string HyperLink
    {
        get { return _HyperLink; }
        set { _HyperLink = value; }
    }
}
#endregion
```

The following code shows the method that displays the orders:

```
#region ShowOrders
private void ShowOrders()
{
    // Create DataContext
    ODataServiceReference.ApplicationData objApplicationData =
        new ODataServiceReference.ApplicationData(
            new Uri(string.Format(@"{0}applicationdata.svc/", BaseSiteUrl)));
    // Query OData source
    var result = from FlowerShopOrders in objApplicationData.FlowerShopOrders
                    .Expand(x => x.FlowerShopCustomer)
                    .Expand(x => x.FlowerShopOrderDetail)
                select FlowerShopOrders;
    // Collection to hold Orders
    List<OrderInfo> colOrderInfo = new List<OrderInfo>();
    // Loop thru orders
    foreach (var item in result)
    {
        // Get the Order Total
        double dblOrderTotal = 0.00d;
        // Create a new DataContext
        ODataServiceReference.ApplicationData objApplicationData2 =
            new ODataServiceReference.ApplicationData(
                new Uri(string.Format(@"{0}applicationdata.svc/", BaseSiteUrl)));
        // Query OData source
        var objOrderDetails = from OrderDetails in objApplicationData2.FlowerShopOrderDetails
                            .Expand(x => x.FlowerShopProduct)
                            where OrderDetails.FlowerShopOrder.Id == item.Id
                            select OrderDetails;
        // Loop thru order details to get order total
        foreach (var OrderDetail in objOrderDetails)
        {
            dblOrderTotal = dblOrderTotal
                + Convert.ToDouble((OrderDetail.FlowerShopProduct.Price * OrderDetail.Quantity));
        }
        // Create new Order object
        OrderInfo objOrderInfo = new OrderInfo();
        objOrderInfo.OrderID = item.Id;
        objOrderInfo.OrderName =
            String.Format("[{0}] {1}, {2} - ${3}",
            item.Id,
            item.FlowerShopCustomer.LastName,
            item.FlowerShopCustomer.FirstName,
            dblOrderTotal);
        objOrderInfo.OrderDate = item.OrderDate;
        objOrderInfo.HyperLink = String.Format(@"OrderEdit.aspx?Id={0}", item.Id);
        // Add the order object to the final collection
        colOrderInfo.Add(objOrderInfo);
    }
    // Bind entire collection to GridView
    gvOrders.DataSource = colOrderInfo;
    gvOrders.DataBind();
}
#endregion
```

The Order Edit Page

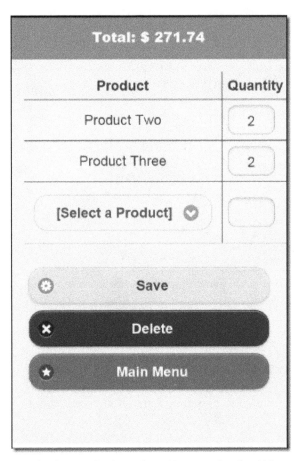

The **OrderEdit.aspx** page displays a single order, allows order detail items to be added, and orders to be deleted.

The code for the **OrderEdit.aspx** page starts with references to add **jQuery Mobile**, and set the page styling:

```
<%@ Page Language="C#" AutoEventWireup="true" CodeBehind="OrderEdit.aspx.cs"
    Inherits="LightSwitchApplication.Mobile.OrderEdit" %>
<!DOCTYPE html>
<html>
<head>
    <title>Order Details</title>
    <meta charset="utf-8">
    <meta name="viewport" content="width=device-width, initial-scale=1">
    <link rel="stylesheet" href="http://code.jquery.com/mobile/1.0.1/jquery.mobile-1.0.1.min.css" />
    <script src="http://code.jquery.com/jquery-1.6.4.min.js"></script>
    <script src="http://code.jquery.com/mobile/1.0.1/jquery.mobile-1.0.1.min.js"></script>
    <style type="text/css">
        table
        {
            width: 100%;
        }
        table caption
        {
            text-align: center;
        }
        table thead th
        {
            text-align: left;
            border-bottom-width: 1px;
            border-top-width: 1px;
        }
        table th, td
        {
            text-align: center;
            padding: 6px;
        }
        ul
        {
            width: 100%;
            margin-left: 0px;
            padding: 0px;
        }
        ul li
        {
            list-style-type: none;
            border-bottom: 1px dashed gray;
            margin-top: 10px;
        }
    </style>
</head>
```

The following shows the remainder of the markup for the page:

```
<body>
    <form id="form1" runat="server">
    <div data-role="page" class="type-interior">
        <div data-role="header" data-theme="b">
            <h1>
            <asp:label id="lblOrderHeader" runat="server" />
            </h1>
        </div>
        <!-- /header -->
        <div data-role="content">
            <asp:gridview id="gvOrderDetails" runat="server" autogeneratecolumns="False"
                datakeynames="Id" horizontalalign="Center" data-role="fieldcontain"
                ShowFooter="True">
                <Columns>
                    <asp:TemplateField HeaderText="Product" ItemStyle-HorizontalAlign="Left">
                        <FooterTemplate>
                            <asp:DropDownList ID="dllProducts" runat="server" data-native-menu="false" />
                        </FooterTemplate>
                        <ItemTemplate>
                            <asp:Label ID="lblId" runat="server" Text='<%# Bind("Id") %>' Visible="False" />
                            <asp:Label ID="lblProduct" runat="server" Text='<%# Bind("Product") %>' />
                        </ItemTemplate>
                        <HeaderStyle HorizontalAlign="Center" />
                        <ItemStyle HorizontalAlign="Left" Width="90%" />
                    </asp:TemplateField>
                    <asp:TemplateField HeaderText="Quantity" ItemStyle-HorizontalAlign="Center">
                        <FooterTemplate>
                            <asp:TextBox ID="txtInsertQuantity" runat="server" Columns="2" data-mini="true"
                                MaxLength="3" style="text-align: center" Text='<%# Bind("Quantity") %>'
                                type="number" Width="40px" />
                        </FooterTemplate>
                        <ItemTemplate>
                            <asp:TextBox ID="txtQuantity" runat="server" Text='<%# Bind("Quantity") %>'
                                Columns="2" data-mini="true" MaxLength="3" Width="40px" type="number"
                                style="text-align: center" />
                        </ItemTemplate>
                        <HeaderStyle HorizontalAlign="Center" />
                        <ItemStyle HorizontalAlign="Center" />
                    </asp:TemplateField>
                </Columns>
                <EmptyDataTemplate>
                    No records found
                </EmptyDataTemplate>
            </asp:gridview>
            <asp:Label ID="lblError" runat="server" ForeColor="Red"
                ViewStateMode="Disabled"></asp:Label>
            <br />
            <asp:Button ID="btnSave" runat="server" Text="Save" data-icon="gear"
                data-role="button" data-ajax="false" data-theme="e" OnClick="btnSave_Click" />
            <asp:Button ID="btnDelete" runat="server" Text="Delete" data-icon="delete"
                data-role="button" data-ajax="false" data-theme="a"
                OnClientClick='if (!confirm("Are you sure you want to delete?") ){return false;}'
                OnClick="btnDelete_Click" />
            <asp:hyperlink id="lnkMainMenu" runat="server" navigateurl="~/MobileMenu.aspx" data-role="button"
                data-ajax="false" data-icon="star" data-theme="b" text="Main Menu" />
        </div>
        <!-- /content -->
    </div>
    <!-- /page -->
    </form>
</body>
</html>
```

We will now examine the code behind. First, we have the imports and a property that provides the base URL for the application:

```
using System;
using System.Collections.Generic;
using System.IO;
using System.Linq;
using System.Web;
using System.Web.UI;
using System.Web.UI.WebControls;
using System.Xml.Linq;
namespace LightSwitchApplication.Mobile
{
    public partial class OrderEdit : System.Web.UI.Page
    {
        #region BaseSiteUrl
        public static string BaseSiteUrl
        {
            get
            {
                HttpContext context = HttpContext.Current;
                string baseUrl = context.Request.Url.Scheme
                    + "://"
                    + context.Request.Url.Authority
                    + context.Request.ApplicationPath.TrimEnd('/') + '/';
                return baseUrl;
            }
        }
        #endregion
```

We also have a class that is used to display the order details:

```
#region OrderDetailsInfo
public class OrderDetailsInfo
{
    int _Id;
    public int Id
    {
        get { return _Id; }
        set { _Id = value; }
    }
    string _Product;
    public string Product
    {
        get { return _Product; }
        set { _Product = value; }
    }
    int _Quantity;
    public int Quantity
    {
        get { return _Quantity; }
        set { _Quantity = value; }
    }
}
#endregion
```

Next, we have the **Page_Load** method that executes the main methods that display the order details, and fills the products dropdown:

```
protected void Page_Load(object sender, EventArgs e)
{
    if (!Page.IsPostBack)
    {
        // Display Order Details
        LoadOrder();
        // Populate the dropdown
        PopulateProducts();
    }
}
```

There are two methods to handle loading the order details. The first method is used to retrieve the order Id that is being passed in the query string in the URL, and the second method is used to load the order details:

```
#region LoadOrder
private void LoadOrder()
{
    if (this.Request.QueryString["Id"] != null)
    {
        // Load the order based on the Id passed
        LoadOrder(Convert.ToInt32(this.Request.QueryString["Id"]));
    }
}
#endregion
#region LoadOrder(int Id)
private void LoadOrder(int Id)
{
    // Create DataContext
    ODataServiceReference.ApplicationData objApplicationData =
        new ODataServiceReference.ApplicationData(
            new Uri(string.Format(@"{0}applicationdata.svc/", BaseSiteUrl)));
    // Collection to hold Order Details
    var OrderDetailsInfo = new List<OrderDetailsInfo>();
    // Value to hold Order Total
    double dblOrderTotal = 0.00d;
    // Query OData source
    var objOrderDetails = from OrderDetails in objApplicationData.FlowerShopOrderDetails
                          .Expand(x => x.FlowerShopProduct)
                where OrderDetails.FlowerShopOrder.Id == Id
                select OrderDetails;
    foreach (var item in objOrderDetails)
    {
        // Create OrderDetails object
        OrderDetailsInfo NewOrderDetailsInfo = new OrderDetailsInfo();
        // Set values
        NewOrderDetailsInfo.Id = item.Id;
        NewOrderDetailsInfo.Product = item.FlowerShopProduct.ProductName;
        NewOrderDetailsInfo.Quantity = item.Quantity;
        // Add Order Detail to final collection
        OrderDetailsInfo.Add(NewOrderDetailsInfo);
        // Update order total
        dblOrderTotal = dblOrderTotal +
            Convert.ToDouble((item.FlowerShopProduct.Price * item.Quantity));
    }
    // Bind collection to Grid
    gvOrderDetails.DataSource = OrderDetailsInfo;
    gvOrderDetails.DataBind();
    // Display the total
    lblOrderHeader.Text = String.Format("Total: $ {0}", dblOrderTotal);
}
```

The following code is used to display the data for the products dropdown:

```
#region PopulateProducts
private void PopulateProducts()
{
    if (gvOrderDetails.FooterRow != null)
    {
        // Create DataContext
        ODataServiceReference.ApplicationData objApplicationData =
            new ODataServiceReference.ApplicationData(
                new Uri(string.Format(@"{0}applicationdata.svc/", BaseSiteUrl)));
        // Query OData source
        var colFlowerShopProducts = from FlowerShopProducts in objApplicationData.FlowerShopProducts
                                    select FlowerShopProducts;
        // Get an instance of the Dropdown
        DropDownList dllProducts = (DropDownList)gvOrderDetails.FooterRow.FindControl("dllProducts");
        // Bind items to Dropdown
        dllProducts.Items.Clear();
        dllProducts.DataSource = colFlowerShopProducts;
        dllProducts.DataValueField = "Id";
        dllProducts.DataTextField = "ProductName";
        dllProducts.Attributes.Add("data-overlay-theme", "b");
        dllProducts.DataBind();
        // Create default entry to top of Dropdown
        var objListItem = new ListItem("[Select a Product]", "0");
        objListItem.Attributes.Add("data-placeholder", "true");
        dllProducts.Items.Insert(0, objListItem);
        dllProducts.Items.FindByText("[Select a Product]").Selected = true;
        // Add JQuery Mobile attribute to items in Dropdown
        for (int i = 0; i < dllProducts.Items.Count; i++)
        {
            dllProducts.Items[i].Attributes.Add("title", dllProducts.Items[i].Text);
        }
    }
}
#endregion
```

The method to save order details is rather large, so we will look at it in two parts. The first part updates existing order details:

```
protected void btnSave_Click(object sender, EventArgs e)
{
    try
    {
        // Get OrderID
        int intId = Convert.ToInt32(this.Request.QueryString["Id"]);
        // Create DataContext
        ODataServiceReference.ApplicationData objApplicationData =
            new ODataServiceReference.ApplicationData(
                new Uri(string.Format(@"{0}applicationdata.svc/", BaseSiteUrl)));
        #region Existing Order Details
        // Loop thru the Orders in the Grid
        var DataObject = gvOrderDetails.DataSourceObject;
        for (int i = 0; i < gvOrderDetails.Rows.Count; i++)
        {
            // Get an instance of the Label and the TextBox
            Label lblId = (Label)gvOrderDetails.Rows[i].Cells[0].FindControl("lblId");
            TextBox txtQuantity = (TextBox)gvOrderDetails.Rows[i].Cells[0].FindControl("txtQuantity");
            // Convert the Label and the TextBox to values
            int intOrderDetailId = Convert.ToInt32(lblId.Text);
            int intQuantity = Convert.ToInt32(txtQuantity.Text);
            // Query OData source
            var objOrderDetail = (from OrderDetails in objApplicationData.FlowerShopOrderDetails
                                    .Expand(x => x.FlowerShopProduct)
                                  where OrderDetails.Id == intOrderDetailId
                                  select OrderDetails).FirstOrDefault();
            if (objOrderDetail != null)
            {
                // If Quantity is set to zero delete the Product entry
                if (intQuantity == 0)
                {
                    objApplicationData.DeleteObject(objOrderDetail);
                }
                else // Update the Product entry
                {
                    objOrderDetail.Quantity = intQuantity;
                    objApplicationData.UpdateObject(objOrderDetail);
                }
            }
        }
    }
    #endregion
```

The second part inserts a new order detail:

```
            #region New Order Details
            // Get an instance of the Dropdown
            DropDownList dllProducts = (DropDownList)gvOrderDetails.FooterRow.FindControl("dllProducts");
            TextBox txtInsertQuantity = (TextBox)gvOrderDetails.FooterRow.FindControl("txtInsertQuantity");
            // Convert the Label and the TextBox to values
            string strProduct = dllProducts.SelectedItem.Text;
            int intProduct = Convert.ToInt32(dllProducts.SelectedValue);
            int intInsertQuantity = 0;
            // Only try an insert if txtInsertQuantity is an integer
            if (int.TryParse(txtInsertQuantity.Text, out intInsertQuantity))
            {
                if (intProduct != 0 && intInsertQuantity > 0)
                {
                    // Create a new FlowerShopOrderDetail
                    LightSwitchApplication.ODataServiceReference.FlowerShopOrderDetail objFlowerShopOrderDetail =
                        new LightSwitchApplication.ODataServiceReference.FlowerShopOrderDetail();
                    // Set values
                    objFlowerShopOrderDetail.OrderDetail_Order = intId;
                    objFlowerShopOrderDetail.OrderDetail_Product = intProduct;
                    objFlowerShopOrderDetail.Quantity = intInsertQuantity;
                    // Add new FlowerShopOrderDetail
                    objApplicationData.AddToFlowerShopOrderDetails(objFlowerShopOrderDetail);
                }
            }
            #endregion
            // Save all changes as a single Batch call
            objApplicationData.SaveChanges(System.Data.Services.Client.SaveChangesOptions.Batch);
            // Go To Main Menu
            Server.Transfer("MobileMenu.aspx");
        }
        catch (Exception ex)
        {
            ShowError(ex);
            return;
        }
    }
}
#endregion
```

The following method handles deleting an order:

```
#region btnDelete_Click
protected void btnDelete_Click(object sender, EventArgs e)
{
    if (this.Request.QueryString["Id"] != null)
    {
        try
        {
            // Load the order based on the Id passed
            int intId = Convert.ToInt32(this.Request.QueryString["Id"]);
            // Create DataContext
            ODataServiceReference.ApplicationData objApplicationData =
                new ODataServiceReference.ApplicationData(
                    new Uri(string.Format(@"{0}applicationdata.svc/", BaseSiteUrl)));
            // Get all the Order details
            var colOrderDetails = from OrderDetails in objApplicationData.FlowerShopOrderDetails
                                    .Expand(x => x.FlowerShopOrder)
                                    where OrderDetails.FlowerShopOrder.Id == intId
                                    select OrderDetails;
            foreach (var item in colOrderDetails)
            {
                // Delete the Order detail item
                objApplicationData.DeleteObject(item);
            }
            objApplicationData.SaveChanges(System.Data.Services.Client.SaveChangesOptions.Batch);
            // Get the Order
            var objOrder = (from FlowerShopOrders in objApplicationData.FlowerShopOrders
                            where FlowerShopOrders.Id == intId
                            select FlowerShopOrders).FirstOrDefault();
            if (objOrder != null)
            {
                // Delete the Order detail item
                objApplicationData.DeleteObject(objOrder);
                objApplicationData.SaveChanges(System.Data.Services.Client.SaveChangesOptions.Batch);
            }
            // Return to Main Menu
            Server.Transfer("MobileMenu.aspx");
        }
        catch (Exception ex)
        {
            ShowError(ex);
        }
    }
}
#endregion
```

Lastly, the following method displays any errors:

```
// Utility
#region ShowError(Exception ex)
private void ShowError(Exception ex)
{
    // see: http://msdn.microsoft.com/en-us/magazine/hh580732.aspx
    if (ex.InnerException != null)
    {
        // This is a complex error
        var sr = new StringReader(ex.InnerException.Message);
        using (sr)
        {
            XElement root = XElement.Load(sr);
            IEnumerable<XElement> message =
                from el in root.Elements()
                where el.Name.LocalName == "message"
                select el;
            foreach (XElement el in message)
            {
                lblError.Text = String.Format(@"{0}<br />", el.Value);
            }
        }
        sr.Close();
    }
    else
    {
        // This is a simple error -- just show Message
        lblError.Text = String.Format(@"{0}", ex.Message);
    }
}
#endregion
```

Chapter 6: Using Client Side Code (jQuery / datajs / Knockout)

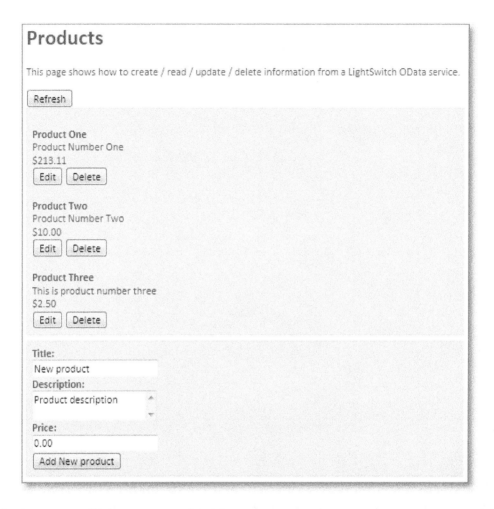

In this chapter we will demonstrate using **jQuery**, **datajs** and **Knockout** to create a page that will cover **C**reating, **R**eading, **U**pdating, and **D**eleting data (also known as **CRUD**).

Some may find that communication with LightSwitch is easier when using server side code. However, an advantage of using client-side JavaScript is:

- You do not need to create an OData service reference (you call the service directly)
- You can place the code in a normal html page

This disadvantage is that the code does not compile at *design-time*, and a small typo can cause the page not to work.

(Note: The following code can be downloaded from the LightSwitchHelpWebsite.com download page at the link titled: *A Full CRUD datajs and KnockoutJs LightSwitch Example Using Only An .Html Page*)

The HTML Page

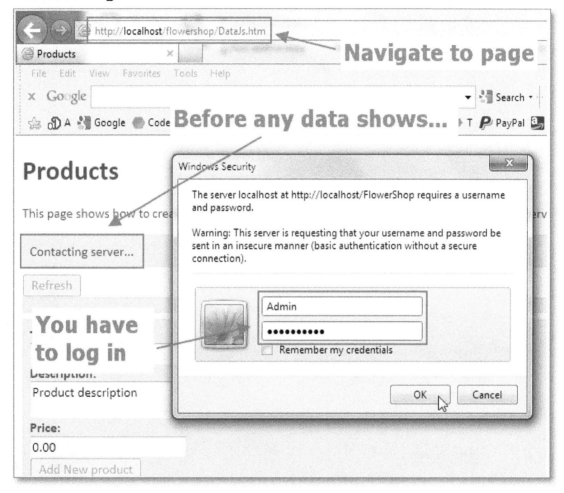

When we run the application and navigate to the page, security is enforced.

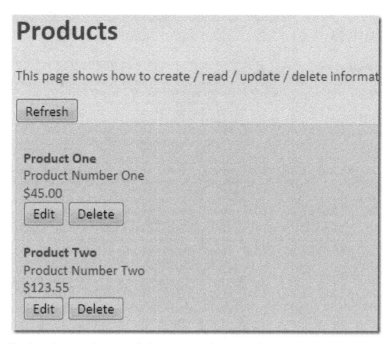

The page will display the products and the **Edit** and **Delete** buttons to any valid user.

Products

This page shows how to cr[...]

Message from webpage ✕

⚠ Error while contacting server: HTTP request failed - {"message":"HTTP request failed","request":{"requestUri":"http://localhost/FlowerShop/ApplicationData.svc/FlowerShopProducts(1)","headers":{"If-Match":"*","Accept":"application/atomsvc+xml;q=0.8, application/json;q=0.5, */*;q=0.1","DataServiceVersion":"1.0","Content-Type":"application/json"},"method":"PUT","data":{"__metadata":{"id":"http://localhost/FlowerShop/ApplicationData.svc/FlowerShopProducts(1)","uri":"http://localhost/FlowerShop/ApplicationData.svc/FlowerShopProducts(1)","etag":"W/\"'Product%20One','Product%20Number%20One',45.00M\"","type":"LightSwitchApplication.FlowerShopProduct"},"FlowerShopOrderDetail":{"__deferred":{"uri":"http://localhost/FlowerShop/ApplicationData.svc/FlowerShopProducts(1)/FlowerShopOrderDetail"}},"Id":1,"ProductName":"Product One","Description":"Product Number One!","Price":"45.00"},"recognizeDates":false,"callbackParameterName":"$callback","formatQueryString":"$format=json","enableJsonpCallback":false,"body":"{\"__metadata\":{\"id\":\"http://localhost/FlowerShop/ApplicationData.svc/FlowerShopProducts(1)\",\"uri\":\"http://localhost/FlowerShop/ApplicationData.svc/FlowerShopProducts(1)\",\"etag\":\"W/\\\"'Product%20One','Product%20Number%20One',45.00M\\\"\",\"type\":\"LightSwitchApplication.FlowerShopProduct\"},\"FlowerShopOrderDetail\":{\"__deferred\":{\"uri\":\"http://localhost/FlowerShop/ApplicationData.svc/FlowerShopProducts(1)/FlowerShopOrderDetail\"}},\"Id\":1,\"ProductName\":\"Product One\",\"Description\":\"Product Number One!\",\"Price\":\"45.00\"}","response":{"requestUri":"http://localhost/FlowerShop/ApplicationData.svc/FlowerShopProducts(1)","statusCode":500,"statusText":"Internal Server Error","headers":[],"body":"{\"error\":{\"code\":\"2\",\"message\":{\"lang\":\"en-US\",\"value\":\"<?xml version=\\\"1.0\\\" encoding=\\\"utf-16\\\"?><ExceptionInfo><Message>The current user does not have permission to update entities in the EntitySet 'FlowerShopProducts'.</Message>...

OK

Refresh

Product One

Product Number One!

45.00

Save   Delete

Product Two
Product Number Two
$123.55
Edit   Delete

Product Three
Product Number Three
$12.32
Edit   Delete

Title:
New product
Description:
Product description

But, if a non-administrator tries to **insert**, **edit** or **delete** records, LightSwitch security in the **OData** service, will enforce all business rules, and in this case prevent the user from performing the action.

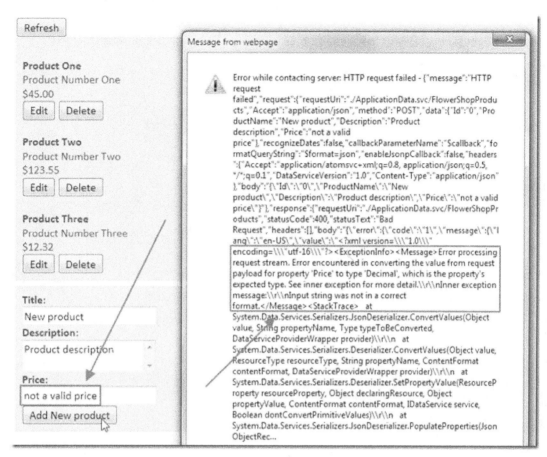

Also, LightSwitch returns *end-user understandable* messages for all validation errors (you will want to parse the entire response to just show the **Message** tags).

datajs and Knockout

The sample application uses **datajs** and **Knockout** (in addition to **jQuery**).

> **datajs** (http://datajs.codeplex.com/) – This **JavaScript** library is used to make the **OData** calls into LightSwitch.

> **Kockout** (http://Knockout.com/) – This **JavaScript** library is used to display the data from **datajs**. It is recommended that you go through these interactive tutorials at: http://learn.Knockout.com/ to understand fully how it works.

LightSwitch OData Security

The sample application consists of a page that allows an administrator to perform **CRUD** operations on the **Product** table in the **Flower Shop** application (used in the previous chapter).

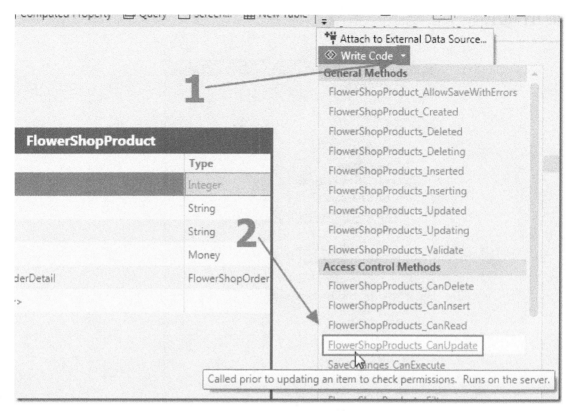

First we need to prevent non-administrators from updating the **Products** entity (table). We open the **Products** entity, and select the **CanUpdate** method. We use the following code:

```
partial void FlowerShopProducts_CanUpdate(ref bool result)
{
    result = this.Application.User.HasPermission(Permissions.SecurityAdministration);
}
```

We do the same for the **CanDelete** and **CanInsert** methods:

```
partial void FlowerShopProducts_CanDelete(ref bool result)
{
    result = this.Application.User.HasPermission(Permissions.SecurityAdministration);
}
partial void FlowerShopProducts_CanInsert(ref bool result)
{
    result = this.Application.User.HasPermission(Permissions.SecurityAdministration);
}
```

The HTML Page

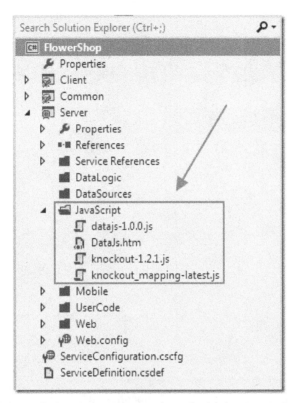

The next thing we do is to switch to **File View** mode and add the **datajs.htm** page and the **.js** files required to support **datajs** and **Knockout** (these are the files that you download from the **datajs** and **Knockout** sites). We also need to unload the LightSwitch project and add the pages to the project manifest. That process is covered in chapter 4.

The Code

Products

This page shows how to create / read / update / delete information from a LightSwitch OData service.

For the top of the **datajs.htm** page we use the following code:

```
<!DOCTYPE html>
<html>
<head>
<title>Products</title>
    <style type="text/css">

    body {
        color: #444444;
        font-family: Calibri, Verdana;
    }
    .titleSpan {
        font-weight: bold;
    }
    .sectionArea {
        border: 1px solid gainsboro;
        padding: 8px;
        margin-bottom: 8px;
        background-color:  #f1edb9;
        width: 50%;
    }
    .ideaBox {
        cursor: pointer;
        padding-top: 8px;
    }
    #modelArea {
        border: 1px solid gainsboro;
        padding: 8px;
        margin-bottom: 8px;
    }
    button, input, textarea { font-family: Calibri, Verdana; font-size: 100%; }
</style>
</head>
<body>
<h1>Products</h1>
<p>
This page shows how to create / read / update / delete information from a LightSwitch OData service.
</p>
```

Contacting server...

Next, we add a **DIV** that will display a message when the page is busy communicating with LightSwitch:

```
<div id='newproductArea' class="sectionArea">
```

Refresh

Then we put in the **Refresh** button. This is a normal **HTML** button except for the **Knockout** attributes that will trigger the "**loadproducts**" **JavaScript** method:

```
<button id="refreshButton" data-bind="click: loadproducts, disable: communicating">Refresh</button>
```

We see that **loadproducts** is a **JavaScript** function that calls the LightSwitch **OData** service:

```
// Discards all products and reloads them from the server.
this.loadproducts = function () {
    makeRequest({ requestUri: serviceUri + "FlowerShopProducts" }, function (data) {
        that.products().splice(0, productsViewModel.products().length);
        $.each(data.results, function (index, value) {
            that.products.push(productModelToViewModel(value));
        });
    });
};
```

This is the **makeRequest** method that the **loadproducts** method invokes:

```
// Make a request, setting the 'communicating' flag.
var makeRequest = function (request, success) {
    productsViewModel.communicating(true);
    $("#messageBar").text("Contacting server...").show();
    return OData.request(request, function (data) {
        productsViewModel.communicating(false);
        $("#messageBar").hide();
        success(data);
    }, function (err) {
        productsViewModel.communicating(false);
        $("#messageBar").hide();
        alert("Error while contacting server: " + err.message + " - " + JSON.stringify(err));
    });
};
```

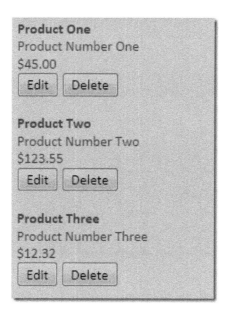

The following is the **DIV** and the template used to display the products:

```
<div id="productsArea"
        data-bind="template: { name: 'productTemplate', foreach: products }"
        class="sectionArea">
</div>
<script type="x-jquery-tmpl" id="productTemplate">
<div class='productBox'>
{{if editing}}
  <input type="text" data-bind="value: ProductName" size="80" /><br />
  <textarea data-bind="value: Description" cols="80" rows="4"></textarea><br />
  <input type="text" data-bind="value: Price" size="80" /><br />
  <button data-bind="click: saveproduct, disable: communicating">Save</button>
{{else}}<br />
  <span class='titleSpan'>${ProductName}</span><br />
    ${Description}<br />
    $${Price}<br />
  <button data-bind="click: editproduct, disable: communicating">Edit</button>
{{/if}}
<button data-bind="click: deleteproduct, disable: communicating">Delete</button>
<br />
</div>
</script>
```

(Notice there are really two possible templates, a **display template**, and an **edit template**, separated by the **{{if editing}}** value)

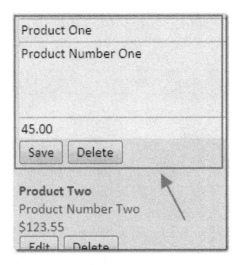

When the **Edit** button is clicked, the following code runs and sets the **editing** flag to true, and the edit template is displayed for the product:

```
// Start editing an product.
model.editproduct = function () {
    this.editing(true);
};
```

When the **Save** button is pressed this code runs:

```
// Save the changes to the product.
model.saveproduct = function () {
    var that = this;
    var data = productViewModelToModel(that);
    var request = {
        requestUri: data.__metadata.uri,
        headers: { "If-Match": " *" },
        method: "PUT",
        data: data
    };
    makeRequest(request, function (data) {
        that.editing(false);
    });
};
```

When the **Delete** button is pressed this code runs:

```
// Deletes this product from the server and removes it from the view model.
model.deleteproduct = function () {
    var that = this;
    var request = {
        requestUri: that.__metadata.uri(),
        headers: { "If-Match": " *" },
        method: "DELETE"
    };
    makeRequest(request, function (data) {
        productsViewModel.products.remove(that);
    });
};
```

When a product is **Inserted**, this code runs:

```
// Adds the newproduct placeholder to the list and saves to the server.
this.addNewproduct = function () {
    var request = {
        requestUri: serviceUri + "FlowerShopProducts",
        Accept: "application/json",
        method: "POST",
        data: {
            Id: that.newproduct.id(),
            ProductName: that.newproduct.productName(),
            Description: that.newproduct.description(),
            Price: that.newproduct.price()
        }
    };
    makeRequest(request, function (newItem) {
        that.newproduct.id("Id");
        that.newproduct.productName("New product");
        that.newproduct.description("Product description");
        that.newproduct.price("Price");
        that.products.push(productModelToViewModel(newItem));
    });
};
```

Chapter 7: A Windows Phone 7 Full CRUD Application

In this chapter, we will create a **Windows Phone 7** application that will cover **C**reating, **R**eading, **U**pdating, and **D**eleting data in LightSwitch using **OData**.

The ODATA Library

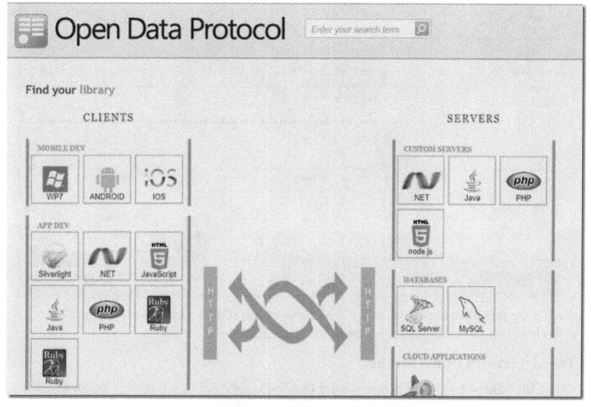

Developing OData clients that communicate with LightSwitch is easy when there is an OData library available to assist you. You can find OData libraries at: http://www.odata.org/libraries.

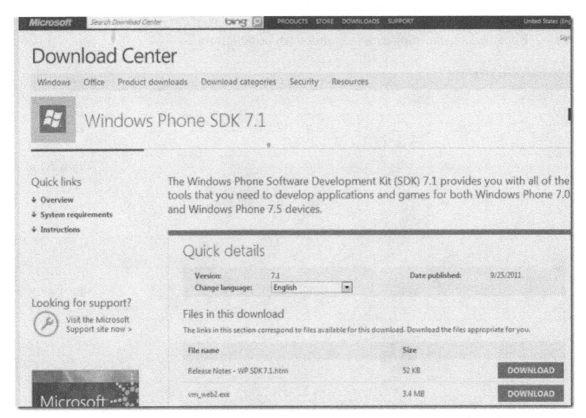

We will use the OData library that is in the Windows Phone SDK. You can download the SDK at this link: http://create.msdn.com/en-us/home/getting_started.

The LightSwitch OData Service

(Note: The following code can be downloaded from the LightSwitchHelpWebsite.com download page at the link titled: *Visual Studio LightSwitch and Windows Phone 7 OData Full CRUD Example*)

LightSwitch OData Security

The sample consists of a page that allows an administrator to perform **CRUD** operations on the **Product** table in the **Flower Shop** application used in the article: Calling LightSwitch 2011 OData Using Server Side Code .

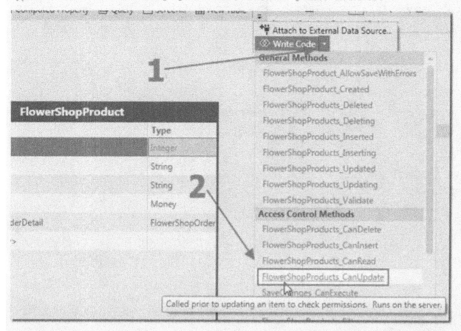

First we need to prevent non-administrators from updating the **Products** entity (table). We open the **Products** entity and select the **CanUpdate** method.

We use the following code:

```
partial void FlowerShopProducts_CanUpdate(ref bool result)
{
    result = this.Application.User.HasPermission(Permissions.SecurityAdministration);
}
```

We do the same for the **CanDelete** and **CanInsert** methods:

```
partial void FlowerShopProducts_CanDelete(ref bool result)
{
    result = this.Application.User.HasPermission(Permissions.SecurityAdministration);
}
partial void FlowerShopProducts_CanInsert(ref bool result)
{
    result = this.Application.User.HasPermission(Permissions.SecurityAdministration);
}
```

We will start with the **Flower Shop** LightSwitch project used in the previous chapter. In that chapter we added security that only allows an administrator the ability to edit the products.

Note: Any security or business rules that you add to the LightSwitch application, are enforced when connecting to the LightSwitch application over OData.

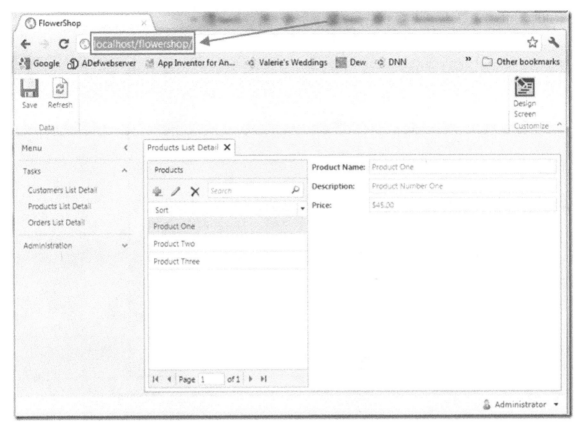

We will publish the LightSwitch application to our local IIS web server so that we can easily connect to it from our Windows Phone 7 application.

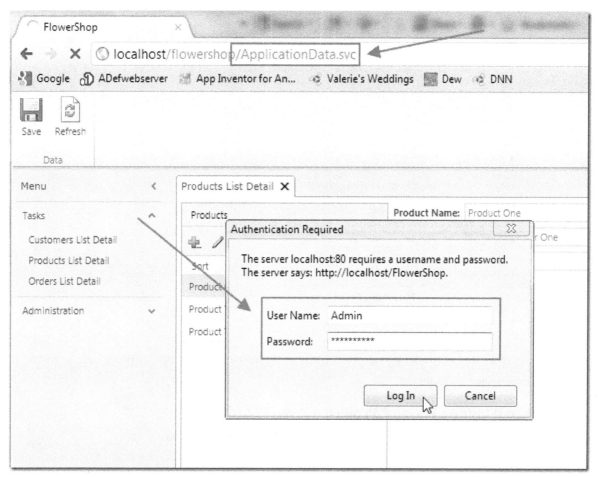

We can navigate to the **OData** service by adding **ApplicationData.svc** to the URL. Because we have enabled security, it will ask us to log in.

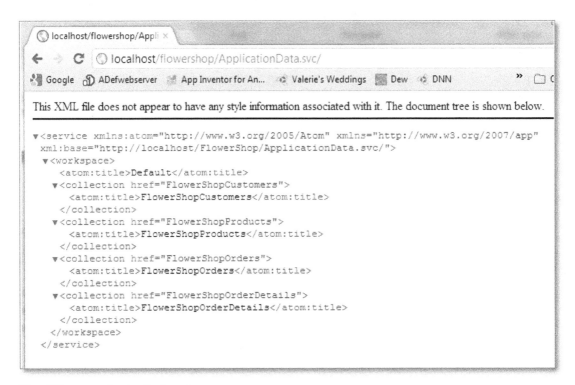

The following XML file does not appear to have any style information associated with it. The document tree is shown below.

```xml
<service xmlns:atom="http://www.w3.org/2005/Atom" xmlns="http://www.w3.org/2007/app"
 xml:base="http://localhost/FlowerShop/ApplicationData.svc/">
  <workspace>
    <atom:title>Default</atom:title>
    <collection href="FlowerShopCustomers">
      <atom:title>FlowerShopCustomers</atom:title>
    </collection>
    <collection href="FlowerShopProducts">
      <atom:title>FlowerShopProducts</atom:title>
    </collection>
    <collection href="FlowerShopOrders">
      <atom:title>FlowerShopOrders</atom:title>
    </collection>
    <collection href="FlowerShopOrderDetails">
      <atom:title>FlowerShopOrderDetails</atom:title>
    </collection>
  </workspace>
</service>
```

The OData service is displayed.

Setup the Windows Phone 7 Project

After installing the latest **Windows Phone SDK**, we open **Visual Studio**.

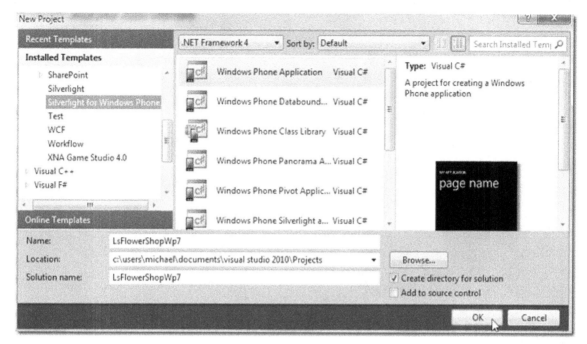

We create a Windows Phone application.

We choose OS 7.1 (or higher).

The project will show.

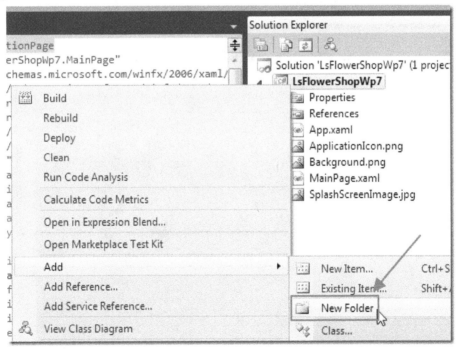

Now, we add a new folder and call it **Images**.

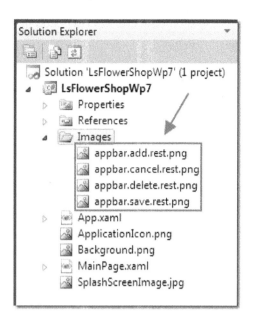

We copy the following images:

appbar.add.rest.png

appbar.cancel.rest.png

appbar.delete.rest.png

appbar.save.rest.png

To the **Images** folder (from the directory created by the **Windows Phone SDK**):

C:\Program Files\Microsoft SDKs\Windows Phone\v7.1\Icons\dark

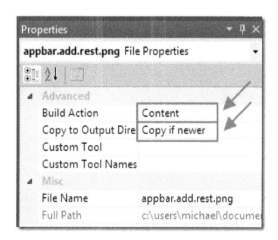

Next, we click on each image and set the **Properties** (to match the image above).

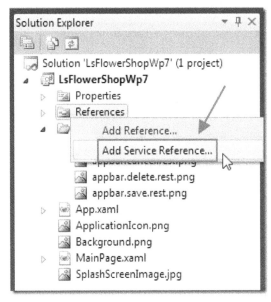

We *right-click* on **References** in the **Solution Explorer**, and we select **Add Service Reference**.

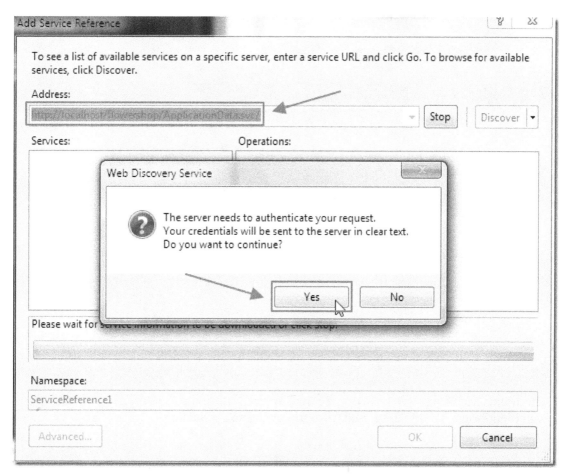

We enter the address to the OData service and click the **Go** button. A box will pop up and ask us to authenticate. We use a LightSwitch account that is an Administrator.

The box may pop up more than once. Enter the same information each time.

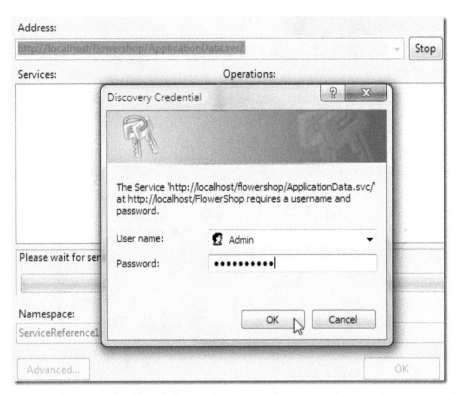

This username and password will only be used to create the proxy class used to communicate with LightSwitch. It will not be used when the application is running.

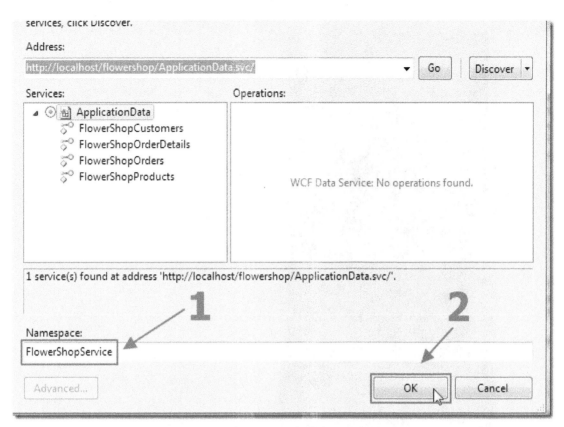

We set the **Namespace** to **FlowerShopService** and click **OK**.

Display List of Entities

We change the content of the **MainPage.xaml** to the following:

```
<phone:PhoneApplicationPage
    x:Class="LsFlowerShopWp7.MainPage"
    xmlns="http://schemas.microsoft.com/winfx/2006/xaml/presentation"
    xmlns:x="http://schemas.microsoft.com/winfx/2006/xaml"
    xmlns:phone="clr-namespace:Microsoft.Phone.Controls;assembly=Microsoft.Phone"
    xmlns:shell="clr-namespace:Microsoft.Phone.Shell;assembly=Microsoft.Phone"
    xmlns:d="http://schemas.microsoft.com/expression/blend/2008"
    xmlns:mc="http://schemas.openxmlformats.org/markup-compatibility/2006"
    mc:Ignorable="d" d:DesignWidth="480" d:DesignHeight="768"
    FontFamily="{StaticResource PhoneFontFamilyNormal}"
    FontSize="{StaticResource PhoneFontSizeNormal}"
    Foreground="{StaticResource PhoneForegroundBrush}"
    SupportedOrientations="Portrait" Orientation="Portrait"
    shell:SystemTray.IsVisible="True">
    <!--LayoutRoot is the root grid where all page content is placed-->
    <Grid x:Name="LayoutRoot" Background="Transparent">
        <Grid.RowDefinitions>
            <RowDefinition Height="Auto"/>
            <RowDefinition Height="*"/>
        </Grid.RowDefinitions>
        <!--TitlePanel contains the name of the application and page title-->
        <StackPanel x:Name="TitlePanel" Grid.Row="0" Margin="12,17,0,28">
            <TextBlock x:Name="ApplicationTitle" Text="LightSwitchHelpWebsite.com"
                    Style="{StaticResource PhoneTextNormalStyle}"/>
            <TextBlock x:Name="PageTitle" Text="Flower Shop" Margin="9,-7,0,0"
                    Style="{StaticResource PhoneTextTitle1Style}"/>
        </StackPanel>
        <!--ContentPanel - place additional content here-->
        <Grid x:Name="ContentPanel" Grid.Row="1" Margin="12,0,12,0">
            <ListBox x:Name="ProductListBox" ItemsSource="{Binding}"
                    SelectionChanged="ProductListBox_SelectionChanged">
                <ListBox.ItemTemplate>
                    <DataTemplate>
                        <StackPanel Orientation="Vertical">
                            <TextBlock Text="{Binding ProductName}"
                    FontSize="{StaticResource PhoneFontSizeExtraLarge}" />
                            <TextBlock Text="{Binding Description}"
                    FontSize="{StaticResource PhoneFontSizeSmall}" />
                            <TextBlock Text="{Binding Price, StringFormat=\{0:C2\}}"
                    FontSize="{StaticResource PhoneFontSizeSmall}" />
                        </StackPanel>
                    </DataTemplate>
                </ListBox.ItemTemplate>
            </ListBox>
        </Grid>
    </Grid>
</phone:PhoneApplicationPage>
```

We replace the contents of **MainPage.xaml.cs** with the following code:

```csharp
public partial class MainPage : PhoneApplicationPage
{
    // Url to the OData Service in Visual Studio LighTSwitch
    private static Uri LightSwitchApplicationUri =
        new Uri("http://localhost/flowershop/ApplicationData.svc/");
    // The Data Service Context that encapsulates operations executed against the oData source
    private ApplicationData ApplicationDataContext;
    // The DataService Collection that will contain the Products
    private DataServiceCollection<FlowerShopService.FlowerShopProduct> dsFlowerShopProducts;
    public MainPage()
    {
        InitializeComponent();
    }
    #region OnNavigatedTo
    protected override void OnNavigatedTo(System.Windows.Navigation.NavigationEventArgs e)
    {
        base.OnNavigatedTo(e);
        // Initialize the Data Service Context
        ApplicationDataContext = new ApplicationData(LightSwitchApplicationUri);
        // Pass the user name and password for the LightSwitch account to be used
        // All security and business logic in LightSwitch will be executed using this account
        ApplicationDataContext.Credentials = new NetworkCredential("Admin", "password#1");
        // The query specifying the data
        var FlowerShopProductsQuery =
            from FlowerShopProducts in ApplicationDataContext.FlowerShopProducts
                            select FlowerShopProducts;
        // Initialize the DataService Collection
        dsFlowerShopProducts =
            new DataServiceCollection<FlowerShopProduct>(ApplicationDataContext);
        // Wire up the dsFlowerShopProducts_LoadCompleted method
        dsFlowerShopProducts.LoadCompleted +=
            new EventHandler<LoadCompletedEventArgs>(dsFlowerShopProducts_LoadCompleted);
        // Start the request to retrieve the data
        dsFlowerShopProducts.LoadAsync(FlowerShopProductsQuery);
    }
    #endregion
    #region dsFlowerShopProducts_LoadCompleted
    void dsFlowerShopProducts_LoadCompleted(object sender, LoadCompletedEventArgs e)
    {
        if (e.Error == null)
        {
            // Check to see if there are multiple pages of data
            if (dsFlowerShopProducts.Continuation != null)
            {
                // Get additional pages of data
                dsFlowerShopProducts.LoadNextPartialSetAsync();
            }
            else
            {
                // Bind the data to the UI
                this.ProductListBox.DataContext = dsFlowerShopProducts;
            }
        }
        else
        {
            // Show any errors
            MessageBox.Show(string.Format("An error has occurred: {0}", e.Error.Message));
        }
    }
    #endregion
    #region ProductListBox_SelectionChanged
    private void ProductListBox_SelectionChanged(object sender, SelectionChangedEventArgs e)
    {
        // Is there an item selected?
        if (null != ProductListBox.SelectedItem)
        {
            // Get the Id of the selected Product
            int Id = (ProductListBox.SelectedItem as FlowerShopService.FlowerShopProduct).Id;
            // Open the EditProduct page passing the Id of the selected Product
            NavigationService.Navigate(
                new Uri(String.Format("/EditProduct.xaml?Id={0}", Id), UriKind.Relative));
        }
    }
    #endregion
```

We hit **F5** to build and run the application.

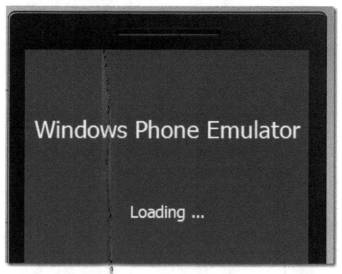

The Windows Phone emulator will start.

The products will display.

Displaying a Single Entity

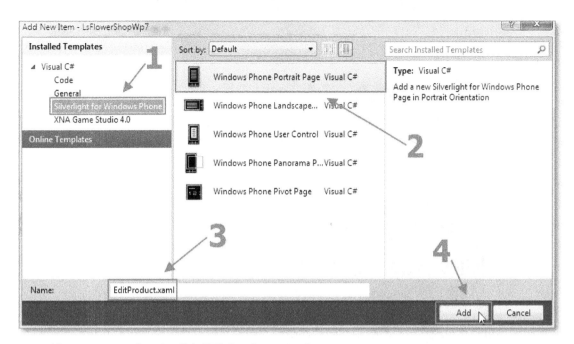

We add a new control and call it **EditProduct.xaml**.

We change the content of **EditProduct.xaml** to the following:

```
<phone:PhoneApplicationPage
    x:Class="LsFlowerShopWp7.EditProduct"
    xmlns="http://schemas.microsoft.com/winfx/2006/xaml/presentation"
    xmlns:x="http://schemas.microsoft.com/winfx/2006/xaml"
    xmlns:phone="clr-namespace:Microsoft.Phone.Controls;assembly=Microsoft.Phone"
    xmlns:shell="clr-namespace:Microsoft.Phone.Shell;assembly=Microsoft.Phone"
    xmlns:d="http://schemas.microsoft.com/expression/blend/2008"
    xmlns:mc="http://schemas.openxmlformats.org/markup-compatibility/2006"
    FontFamily="{StaticResource PhoneFontFamilyNormal}"
    FontSize="{StaticResource PhoneFontSizeNormal}"
    Foreground="{StaticResource PhoneForegroundBrush}"
    SupportedOrientations="Portrait" Orientation="Portrait"
    mc:Ignorable="d" d:DesignHeight="696" d:DesignWidth="480"
    shell:SystemTray.IsVisible="True">
    <!--LayoutRoot is the root grid where all page content is placed-->
    <Grid x:Name="LayoutRoot" Background="Transparent">
        <Grid.RowDefinitions>
            <RowDefinition Height="Auto"/>
            <RowDefinition Height="83*" />
        </Grid.RowDefinitions>
        <!--TitlePanel contains the name of the application and page title-->
        <StackPanel x:Name="TitlePanel" Grid.Row="0" Margin="12,17,0,28">
            <TextBlock x:Name="ApplicationTitle" Text="LightSwitchHelpWebsite.com"
                       Style="{StaticResource PhoneTextNormalStyle}"/>
            <TextBlock x:Name="PageTitle" Text="Flower Shop" Margin="9,-7,0,0"
                       Style="{StaticResource PhoneTextTitle1Style}"/>
        </StackPanel>
        <!--ContentPanel - place additional content here-->
        <Grid x:Name="ContentPanel" Grid.Row="1" Grid.RowSpan="3">
            <Grid.RowDefinitions>
                <RowDefinition Height="90"/>
                <RowDefinition Height="90*" />
                <RowDefinition Height="90*" />
                <RowDefinition Height="90*" />
                <RowDefinition Height="90*" />
                <RowDefinition Height="90*" />
                <RowDefinition Height="63*" />
            </Grid.RowDefinitions>
            <TextBlock Text="Product Name:" Grid.Row="0"
                       HorizontalAlignment="Left" VerticalAlignment="Center" FontSize="40" />
            <TextBox Grid.Row="1" Name="txtProductName"
                     Text="{Binding ProductName, Mode=TwoWay}" Margin="0,0,20,0" />
            <TextBlock Text="Product Description:" Grid.Row="2"
                       HorizontalAlignment="Left" VerticalAlignment="Center" FontSize="40" />
            <TextBox Grid.Row="3" Name="txtProductDescription"
                     Text="{Binding Description, Mode=TwoWay}" Margin="0,0,20,0" />
            <TextBlock Text="Product Price:" Grid.Row="4"
                       HorizontalAlignment="Left" VerticalAlignment="Center" FontSize="40" />
            <TextBox Grid.Row="5" Name="txtProductPrice"
                     Text="{Binding Price, Mode=TwoWay}" Margin="0,0,20,0" Width="150"
                     HorizontalAlignment="Left" />
        </Grid>
    </Grid>
    <phone:PhoneApplicationPage.ApplicationBar>
        <shell:ApplicationBar Mode="Default" Opacity="1.0" IsMenuEnabled="True" IsVisible="True">
            <shell:ApplicationBarIconButton IconUri="/Images/appbar.cancel.rest.png"
                                            Text="cancel" x:Name="btnCancel" Click="btnCancel_Click" />
        </shell:ApplicationBar>
    </phone:PhoneApplicationPage.ApplicationBar>
</phone:PhoneApplicationPage>
```

We use the following code in the **EditProduct.xaml.cs** page:

```
public partial class EditProduct : PhoneApplicationPage
{
    // Url to the OData Service in Visual Studio LighTSwitch
    private static Uri LightSwitchApplicationUri =
        new Uri("http://localhost/flowershop/ApplicationData.svc/");
    // The Data Service Context that encapsulates operations executed against the oData source
    private ApplicationData ApplicationDataContext;
    // The DataService Collection that will contain the Products
    private DataServiceCollection<FlowerShopService.FlowerShopProduct> dsFlowerShopProducts;
    public EditProduct()
    {
        InitializeComponent();
        // Initialize the Data Service Context
        ApplicationDataContext = new ApplicationData(LightSwitchApplicationUri);
        // Pass the user name and password for the LightSwitch account to be used
        // All security and business logic in LightSwitch will be executed using this account
        ApplicationDataContext.Credentials = new NetworkCredential("Admin", "password#1");
    }
    #region OnNavigatedTo
    protected override void OnNavigatedTo(System.Windows.Navigation.NavigationEventArgs e)
    {
        // Thsi method is called when a user navigates to this page
        base.OnNavigatedTo(e);
        string strId;
        // Is an Id passed?
        if (NavigationContext.QueryString.TryGetValue("Id", out strId))
        {
            if (strId != "-1") // An existing Product
            {
                // Convert Id to a integer
                int intId = Convert.ToInt32(strId);
                // Query only the Product matching the Id
                var FlowerShopProductsQuery =
                    from FlowerShopProducts in ApplicationDataContext.FlowerShopProducts
                    where FlowerShopProducts.Id == intId
                    select FlowerShopProducts;
                // Start the process to load the selected Product
                // Initialize the DataService Collection
                dsFlowerShopProducts =
                    new DataServiceCollection<FlowerShopProduct>(ApplicationDataContext);
                // Wire up the dsFlowerShopProducts_LoadCompleted method
                dsFlowerShopProducts.LoadCompleted +=
                    new EventHandler<LoadCompletedEventArgs>(dsFlowerShopProducts_LoadCompleted);
                // Start the request to retrieve the data
                dsFlowerShopProducts.LoadAsync(FlowerShopProductsQuery);
            }
        }
    }
    #endregion
    #region dsFlowerShopProducts_LoadCompleted
    void dsFlowerShopProducts_LoadCompleted(object sender, LoadCompletedEventArgs e)
    {
        if (e.Error == null)
        {
            if (dsFlowerShopProducts.FirstOrDefault() != null)
            {
                // Display the selected Product
                this.ContentPanel.DataContext = dsFlowerShopProducts.FirstOrDefault();
            }
        }
        else
        {
            // Display any errors
            MessageBox.Show(string.Format("An error has occurred: {0}", e.Error.Message));
        }
    }
    #endregion
```

We also add the following methods to handle the **Cancel** button and to assist with binding to the **Text Boxes**:

```csharp
    // ApplicationBar Events
    #region btnCancel_Click
    private void btnCancel_Click(object sender, EventArgs e)
    {
        // Go back to main page
        NavigationService.GoBack();
    }
    #endregion
}
#region Extensions
public static class Extensions
{
    #region UpdateBinding
    // From: http://stackoverflow.com/questions/8168861/
    // two-way-databinding-from-textbox-doesnt-update-when-button-in-applicationbar-is
    public static void UpdateBinding(this TextBox textBox)
    {
        // This is an extension method that solves the problem
        // of a user clicking the save button before clicking
        // outside of a TextBox after making a change
        BindingExpression bindingExpression =
                textBox.GetBindingExpression(TextBox.TextProperty);
        if (bindingExpression != null)
        {
            bindingExpression.UpdateSource();
        }
    }
    #endregion
}
#endregion
```

We hit **F5** to build and run the application. We select a product in the list…

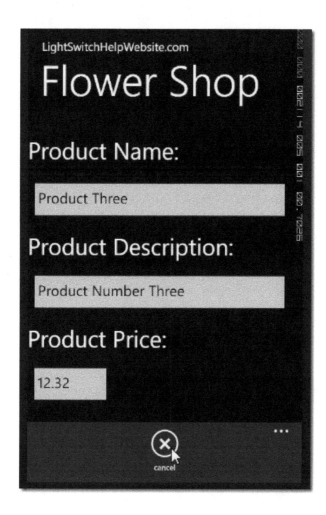

The selected product will display on the **EditProduct.xaml** page. Clicking the **Cancel** button will return to the **MainPage.xaml** page.

Update an Entity

First, we add a button to **EditProduct.xaml**:

```
<shell:ApplicationBarIconButton IconUri="/Images/appbar.save.rest.png" Text="save" x:Name="btnSave"
                                Click="btnSave_Click" />
```

Then, we add the following two methods:

```
#region btnSave_Click
private void btnSave_Click(object sender, EventArgs e)
{
    // Update the bindings on the TextBoxes
    txtProductName.UpdateBinding();
    txtProductDescription.UpdateBinding();
    txtProductPrice.UpdateBinding();
    // Start the saving changes
    ApplicationDataContext.BeginSaveChanges(
        SaveChangesOptions.Batch, OnChangesSaved, ApplicationDataContext);
}
#endregion
#region OnChangesSaved
private void OnChangesSaved(IAsyncResult result)
{
    // Use the Dispatcher to ensure that the
    // asynchronous call returns in the correct thread.
    Dispatcher.BeginInvoke(() =>
    {
        // Cast result to the ApplicationDataContext
        ApplicationDataContext = result.AsyncState as ApplicationData;
        try
        {
            // Complete the save changes operation
            ApplicationDataContext.EndSaveChanges(result);
        }
        catch (Exception ex)
        {
            // Display the error from the response.
            MessageBox.Show(string.Format("An error has occurred: {0}", ex.Message));
        }
        finally
        {
            // Go back to main page
            NavigationService.GoBack();
        }
    });
}
#endregion
```

We hit **F5** to build and run the application.

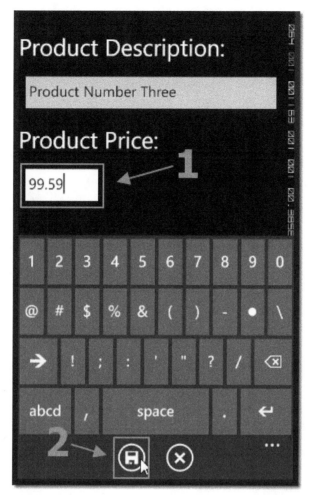

Now, when we edit a product, we can click the **save** button to save the changes, and return to **MainPage.xaml**.

Delete an Entity

First, we add a button to **EditProduct.xaml**:

```
<shell:ApplicationBarIconButton IconUri="/Images/appbar.delete.rest.png"
                                Text="delete" x:Name="btnDelete" Click="btnDelete_Click" />
```

Next we add the following two methods:

```
#region btnDelete_Click
private void btnDelete_Click(object sender, EventArgs e)
{
    // Get the product that is bound to the UI
    FlowerShopProduct ProductToDelete =
        (FlowerShopProduct)this.ContentPanel.DataContext;
    if (ProductToDelete != null)
    {
        // Mark the Product to be deleted
        ApplicationDataContext.DeleteObject(ProductToDelete);
        // Start the request to delete the Product
        ApplicationDataContext.BeginSaveChanges(DeleteProductHandler, ProductToDelete);
    }
}
#endregion
#region DeleteProductHandler
private void DeleteProductHandler(IAsyncResult result)
{
    // Use the Dispatcher to ensure that the
    // asynchronous call returns in the correct thread.
    Dispatcher.BeginInvoke(() =>
    {
        // Cast result to the Product
        FlowerShopProduct ProductToDelete = result.AsyncState as FlowerShopProduct;
        try
        {
            // Delete the Product
            ApplicationDataContext.EndSaveChanges(result);
        }
        catch (Exception ex)
        {
            // Display the error from the response.
            MessageBox.Show(string.Format("An error has occurred: {0}", ex.Message));
        }
        finally
        {
            // Go back to main page
            NavigationService.GoBack();
        }
    });
}
#endregion
```

We hit **F5** to build and run the application.

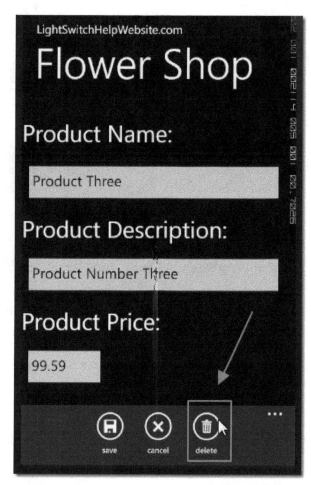

We can click the **delete** button while viewing a product in edit mode, and it will delete it, and return to **MainPage.xaml**.

Note that we will not be allowed to delete a product that has been used in a **Flower Shop** order (also note that there is an inner exception message that clearly indicates this, but the code to parse that inner exception message was verbose so it was not included in this sample to keep the code as simple as possible).

Insert a Entity

First, we add a button to **MainPage.xaml**:

```
<phone:PhoneApplicationPage.ApplicationBar>
    <shell:ApplicationBar Mode="Default" Opacity="1.0"
                          IsMenuEnabled="True" IsVisible="True">
        <shell:ApplicationBarIconButton IconUri="/Images/appbar.add.rest.png"
                          Text="add" x:Name="btnAdd" Click="btnAdd_Click" />
    </shell:ApplicationBar>
</phone:PhoneApplicationPage.ApplicationBar>
```

We add the following method to **MainPage.xaml.cs** that will navigate us to the **EditProduct.xaml** page passing a –1 to indicate that it is a new record:

```
#region btnAdd_Click
private void btnAdd_Click(object sender, EventArgs e)
{
    // Open the EditProduct page passing the Id of -1 to indicate it is a new record
    NavigationService.Navigate(new Uri("/EditProduct.xaml?Id=-1", UriKind.Relative));
}
#endregion
```

On the **EditProduct.xaml.cs** page, we add the following code to the **OnNavigatedTo** method to create a new product when -1 is passed:

```
else // A new Product
{
    // Create a new Product
    FlowerShopProduct objFlowerShopProduct = new FlowerShopProduct();
    // Add the new Product to the Data Service Context
    ApplicationDataContext.AddToFlowerShopProducts(objFlowerShopProduct);
    // Set the context of the UI to the new Product
    this.ContentPanel.DataContext = objFlowerShopProduct;
}
```

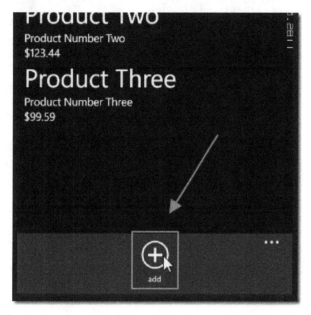

When we run the application, we can click the add button to add a new product.

We enter the product information and click the **save** button.

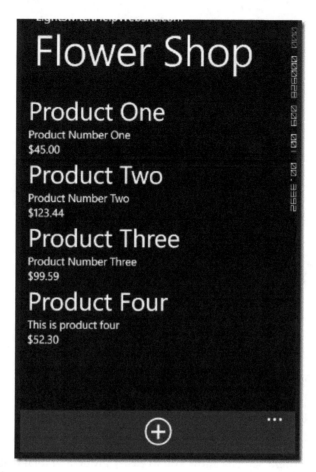

The product is added.

Chapter 8: Shape Your LightSwitch OData Using WCF RIA Services

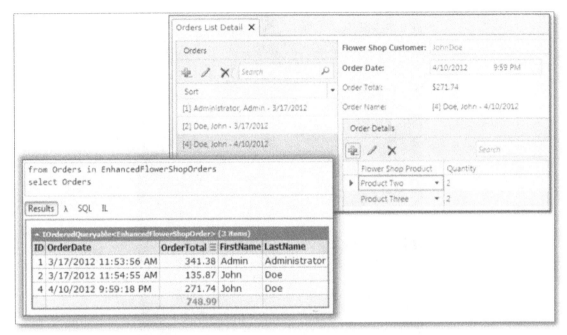

The LightSwitch Silverlight screens allow you to easily group and total data. The LightSwitch **OData** services return one **Entity** collection at a time. This makes grouping and totaling across **Entity** collections difficult. Using **WCF RIA Services** provides a clean elegant solution.

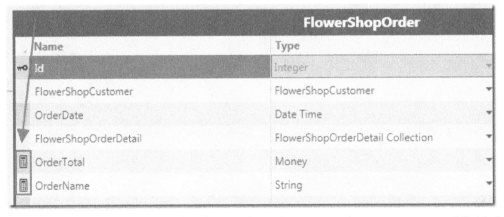

In the **Flower Shop** application used in the previous chapters, we have two computed fields in the **FlowerShopOrder Entity**.

These fields allow us to easily display the **Order Total** and the name of the **Customer**.

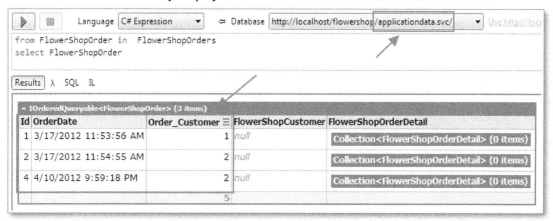

However, if we connect to the **OData** service for that **Entity** using **LinqPad** (you can download **LinqPad** from: http://www.linqpad.net) , we see it does not contain the **Order Total** or the name of the **Customer**.

To get this data, it requires additional queries of **Customer Entity** to get the **Customer** name, the **Product Entity** to get the **Product** price, and all the related **Order Detail Entities** to calculate the **Order Total**.

This is a problem because not only does it require additional database queries, it requires the client consuming the **OData** feed to now be responsible for complex business logic.

We can create an **OData** service with these computed fields using a **WCF RIA Service**.

Create A WCF RIA Service

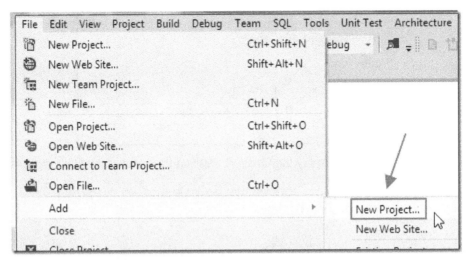

Open up one of the **Flower Shop** applications used in the previous chapters and select **Add** a
New Project.

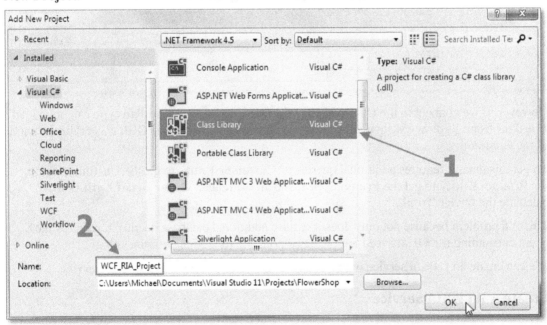

Create a **Class Library** called **WCF_RIA_Project.**

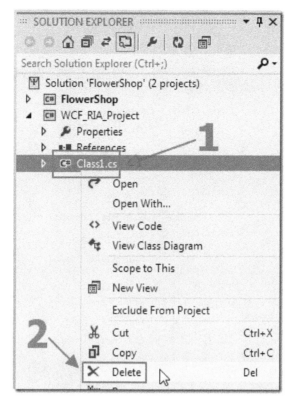

Delete the **Class1.cs** file that is automatically created.

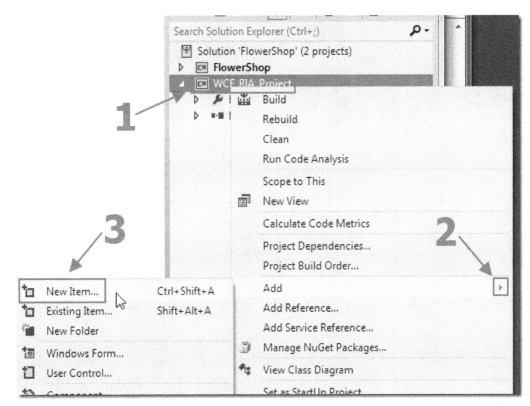

Add a **New Item** to the **WCF_RIA_Project**.

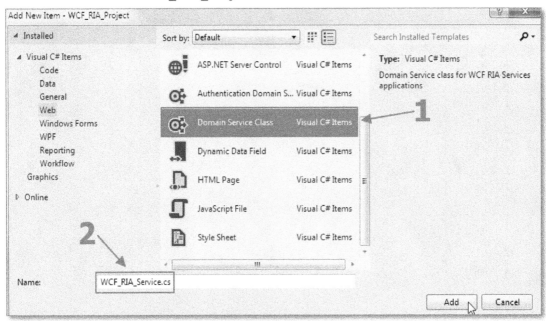

Add a **Domain Service Class** called **WCF_RIA_Service**.

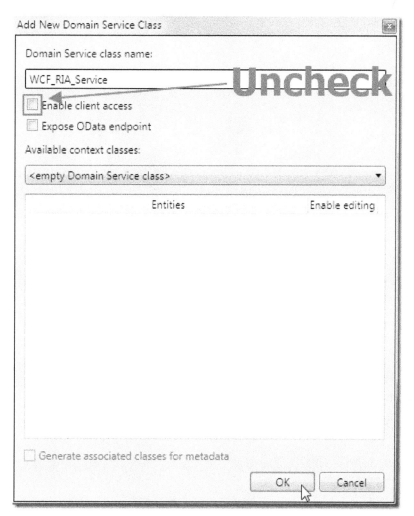

When the **Add New Domain Service Class** box comes up, *uncheck* **Enable client access**. Click **OK** (this domain class will be exposed by LightSwitch, and will pass through its security and business rules).

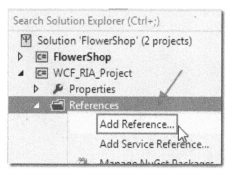

Add the following references to the **WCF_RIA_Project**:

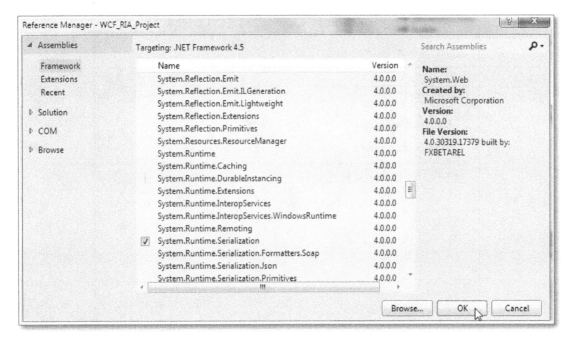

System.ComponentModel.DataAnnotations

System.Configuration

System.Data.Entity

System.Runtime.Serialization

System.Web

System.ServiceModel.DomainServices.Server *(Look in %ProgramFiles%\Microsoft SDKs\RIA Services\v1.0\Libraries\Server)*

Add the following *Using Statements* to the class:

```
 2  namespace WCF_RIA_Project
 3  {
 4      using System;
 5      using System.Collections.Generic;
 6      using System.ComponentModel;
 7      using System.ComponentModel.DataAnnotations;
 8      using System.Linq;
 9      using System.ServiceModel.DomainServices.Hosting;
10      using System.ServiceModel.DomainServices.Server;
11      using ApplicationData.Implementation;
12      using System.Data.EntityClient;
13      using System.Web.Configuration;
14
15
16      // TODO: Create methods containing your application
17      // TODO: add the EnableClientAccessAttribute to this
```

using ApplicationData.Implementation;
using System.Data.EntityClient;
using System.Web.Configuration;

(ApplicationData will display a squiggly red line because the class is missing, but it will be added in a subsequent step)

Reference the LightSwitch Object Context

Now, we will add code from the LightSwitch project to our **WCF RIA Service** project. We will add a class that LightSwitch automatically creates, that connects to the database that LightSwitch uses.

We will use this class in our **WCF RIA Service** to communicate with the LightSwitch database.

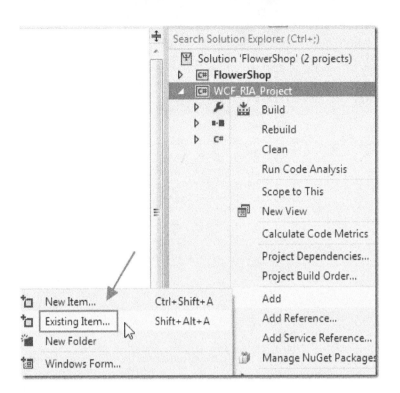

Right-click on the **WCF_RIA_Project** and select **Add** then **Existing Item**.

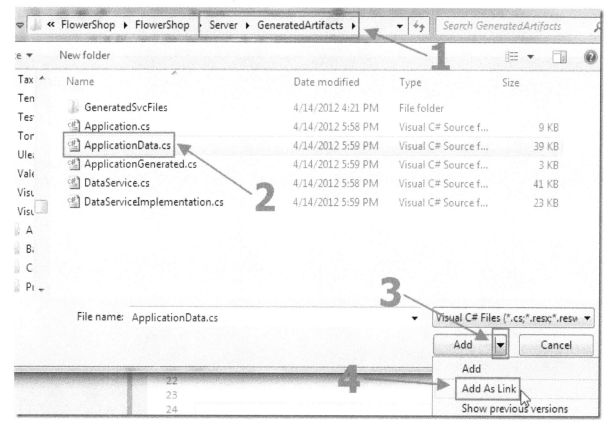

Navigate to ..**Server\GeneratedArtifacts** (in the LightSwitch project) and click on
ApplicationData.cs and **Add As Link**.

We use *add As Link* so our **WCF RIA Service** will be updated when LightSwitch updates this
class. This is how our **WCF RIA Service** will be able to see any new **Entities** (tables) that are
added, deleted, or changed.

Create the Domain Service

We use the following code in the **WCF RIA Service** to set up the database connection and to
create a class that will be used to transfer the data (**EnhancedFlowerShopOrder**):

```
namespace WCF_RIA_Project
{
    using System;
    using System.Collections.Generic;
    using System.ComponentModel;
    using System.ComponentModel.DataAnnotations;
    using System.Linq;
    using System.ServiceModel.DomainServices.Hosting;
    using System.ServiceModel.DomainServices.Server;
    using ApplicationData.Implementation;
    using System.Data.EntityClient;
    using System.Web.Configuration;
    // This class is used as the class that is returned
    // This can have any 'shape' you desire
    // Make sure this is outside of the WCF_RIA_Service class
    // but inside the WCF_RIA_Project namespace
    public class EnhancedFlowerShopOrder
    {
        [Key]
        public int ID { get; set; }
        public DateTime OrderDate { get; set; }
        public string FirstName { get; set; }
        public string LastName { get; set; }
        public decimal OrderTotal { get; set; }
    }
    public class WCF_RIA_Service : DomainService
    {
        // This Context property is code that connects to the LightSwitch database
        // The code in the Database connection region can be reused as it is
        #region Database connection
        private ApplicationDataObjectContext m_context;
        public ApplicationDataObjectContext Context
        {
            get
            {
                if (this.m_context == null)
                {
                    string connString =
                        System.Web.Configuration.WebConfigurationManager
                        .ConnectionStrings["_IntrinsicData"].ConnectionString;
                    EntityConnectionStringBuilder builder = new EntityConnectionStringBuilder();
                    builder.Metadata =
                        "res://*/ApplicationData.csdl|res://*/ApplicationData.ssdl|res://*/ApplicationData.msl";
                    builder.Provider =
                        "System.Data.SqlClient";
                    builder.ProviderConnectionString = connString;
                    this.m_context = new ApplicationDataObjectContext(builder.ConnectionString);
                }
                return this.m_context;
            }
        }
        #endregion
```

We use the following code to implement the query:

```
[Query(IsDefault = true)]
public IQueryable<EnhancedFlowerShopOrder> GetAllOrders()
{
    // Get all the Orders
    var colFlowerShopOrders = from Order in this.Context.FlowerShopOrders
                              // Shape the results into the
                              // EnhancedFlowerShopOrder class
                              select new EnhancedFlowerShopOrder
                              {
                                  // The Order ID
                                  ID = Order.Id,
                                  // The Order Date
                                  OrderDate = Order.OrderDate,
                                  // The first name of the Customer
                                  FirstName = Order.FlowerShopCustomer.FirstName,
                                  // The last name of the Customer
                                  LastName = Order.FlowerShopCustomer.LastName,
                                  // The order Total
                                  OrderTotal =
                                  // Get all order details lines of the Order
                                  (from FlowerShopOrderDetail in Order.FlowerShopOrderDetail
                                   // Group the products in the Order Details
                                   group FlowerShopOrderDetail
                                   by FlowerShopOrderDetail.FlowerShopProduct into g
                                   // Shape a new entity
                                   select new
                                   {
                                       // Create a total property that is the Quantity times the
                                       // Product price
                                       TotalOrder = g.Sum(x => x.Quantity)
                                       * g.Sum(x => x.FlowerShopProduct.Price),
                                   }).Sum(x => x.TotalOrder) // Add the sum of all the TotalOrders
                              };
    return colFlowerShopOrders;
}
// Override the Count method in order for paging to work correctly
protected override int Count<T>(IQueryable<T> query)
{
    return query.Count();
}
```

Consume the WCF RIA Service

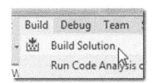

Build the solution. You will see warnings in the immediate window, you can ignore them.

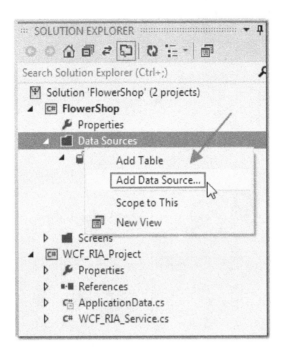

In the **Solution Explorer** (of the LightSwitch project), *right-click* on the **Data Sources** folder and select **Add Data Source**.

Select **WCF RIA Service** and click **Next**.

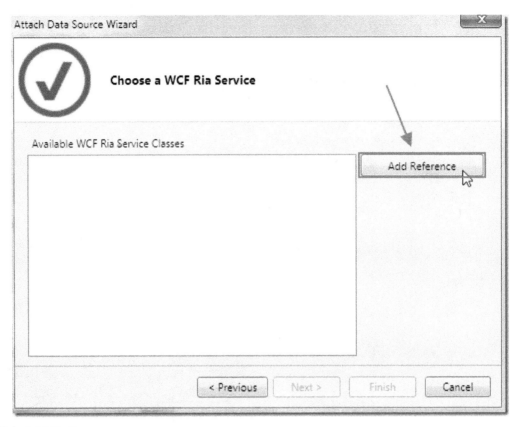

Click **Add Reference**.

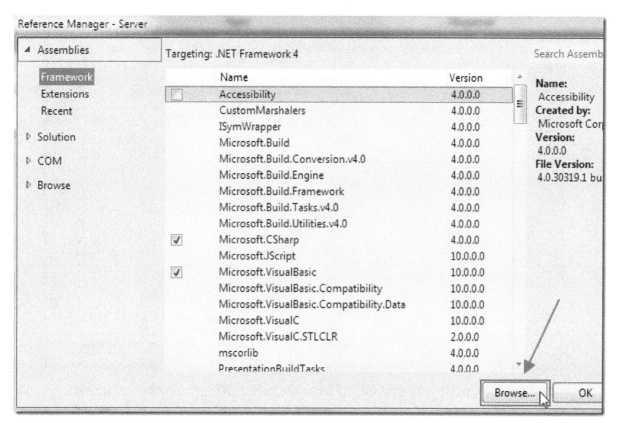

Click **Browse…**

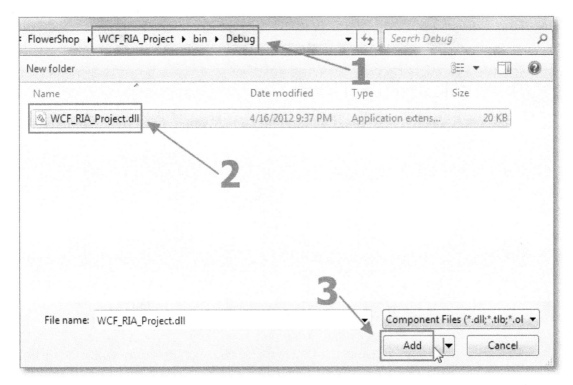

Navigate to the **WCF_RIA_Project.dll** in *FlowerShop/WCF_RIA_Project/bin/debug* and select it.

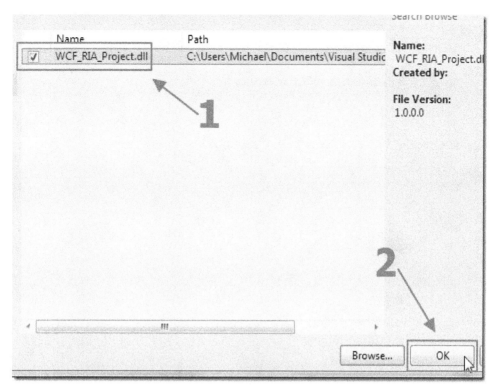

It will display in the dialog box, select it and click **OK**.

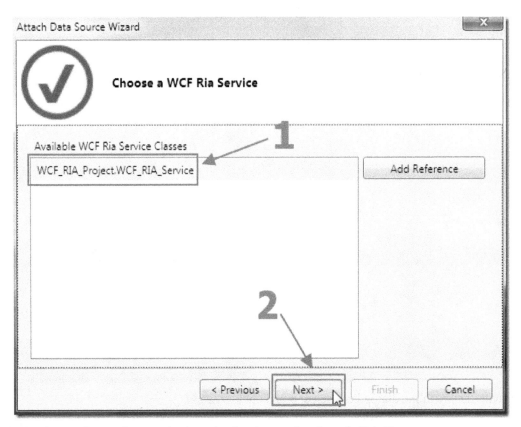

Wait for the service to show up in the selection box, select it and click **Next**.

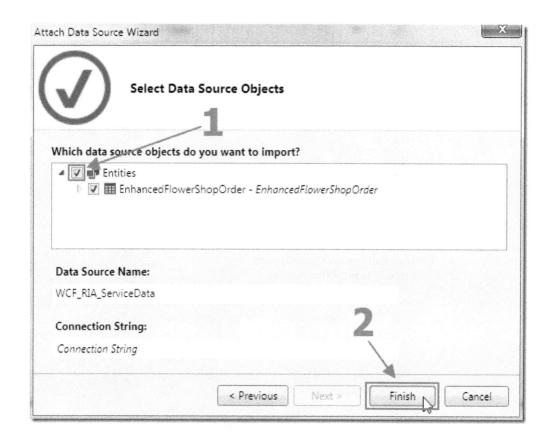

Check the box next to the **Entities**, and click **Finish**.

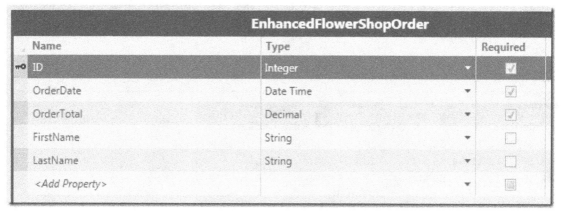

The **Entity** will display.

Display the Data

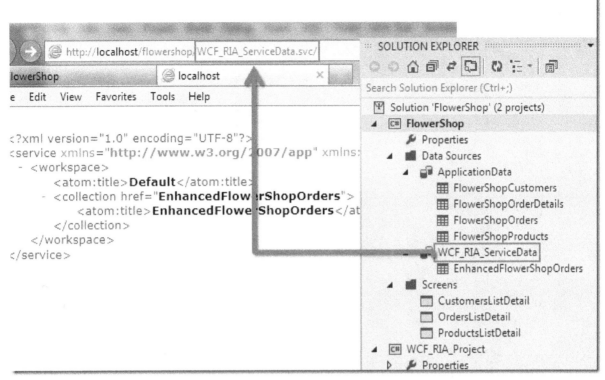

The **WCF RIA Service** will have its own node under **Data Sources** in the LightSwitch project. That name plus ".svc" is used to navigate to the **OData** service.

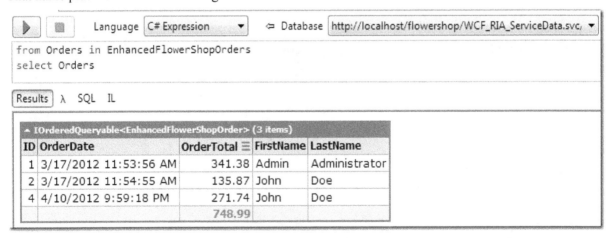

Using **LinqPad** (you can download **LinqPad** from: http://www.linqpad.net), we can now issue a simple query to access the data.

Chapter 9: The Future

One thing I have come to accept over the past two years interacting with the LightSwitch team is that they think ahead. The proof is in the LightSwitch framework and its extensibility that can handle any challenge I have thrown at it.

The LightSwitchHelpWebsite.com has over 50 sample applications that have been created over the past two years. These 50 sample applications prove that LightSwitch is a great platform for enterprise application development.

Implementing OData in LightSwitch is a brilliant decision that allows LightSwitch to communicate with an unlimited variety of clients, servers, and devices. This assures the ability of LightSwitch to grow and adapt to future technological changes.

About The Author

Michael Washington is an ASP.NET, C#, and Visual Basic programmer. He has extensive knowledge in process improvement, billing systems, and student information systems. He is a Microsoft Silverlight MVP. He has a son, Zachary and resides in Los Angeles with his wife Valerie.

He has written over 50 Visual Studio LightSwitch tutorials at:
http://lightswitchhelpwebsite.com/Blog.aspx.

He is the author of three previous books:

- **Creating Visual Studio LightSwitch Custom Controls (Beginner to Intermediate)** (LightSwitchHelpWebsite.com)
- **Building Websites with VB.NET and DotNetNuke 4** (Packt Publishing)
- **Building Websites with DotNetNuke 5** (Packt Publishing)